Motivational Spirit

How to Keep Yours Solid as a Rock!

Robert Kirby

The Genesis of
My Motivational Spirit:

W.V. State Bodybuilding Championship 1991

First published by Dog Ear Publishing
4011 Vincennes Road
Indianapolis, IN 46268
www.dogearpublishing.net

ISBN: 978-145756-714-8

This book is printed on acid-free paper.
Printed in the United States of America

TABLE OF CONTENTS

INTRODUCTION

"Keep your mind open to change all the time. Welcome it. Court it. It's only by examining and reexamining your opinions and ideas that you can progress." —Dale Carnegie

The distinctive features of this book are the cohesiveness and complimentary nature of the motivational ingredients; its wide-ranging, insightful research; and the *chunking* style I utilize to convey the material.

The reality is, there are limits to the number of concepts that can be held in our minds at one time; therefore, the fewer we hold in our thoughts at once the better. When we are able to reduce complex ideas to a couple of concepts, it then becomes much easier to manipulate and remember the concepts in our minds. The ability to simplify complex concepts into their essential elements is a positive habit that the majority of highly successful business executives have used to keep their motivational spirit solid as a rock. This ability to simplify and breakdown concepts is a skill called *chunking*. [1]

The following experiment is an example of chunking: Take 10 seconds to memorize these 10 digits: 1659326541. How well did you do at this little experiment…was it easy? Next, try memorizing a new set of digits for 10 seconds, 2134176594, but for this set, do it by chunking the numbers into pairs: 21 34 17 65 94. If you timed yourself, you would quickly become aware of how much simpler and more efficient it is to memorize the second set of numbers. Numerous studies, including those conducted by Professor Fernand Gobet at Brunel University located in the UK, highlight the fact that our brains learn multifaceted sequences by automatically sorting information into chunks. The size of the chunk of information roughly correlates to the amount of time it takes you to say each item—in this case, numbers. Importantly noted, the most efficient chunks of information take less than 2 seconds to repeat out loud or think about. The fact is, the human brain wants to chunk information anytime we reach the limits of what can be effectively processed and retained.[1]

When we create a habit of chunking information, subsequently patterns of knowledge emerge, thus increasing our awareness of specific information we need to know. Possessing a clear understanding of the chunking process rather than simply doing it indirectly will assist you in utilizing this learning tool more often, as well as more efficiently.

Simplicity provides us with a greater sense of certainty. This is why I highlight the topic of chunking because *certainty* is a topic that I discuss in this book; it is vitally important to keeping our motivational spirit vibrant. Also, throughout the writing of this book, the concept of chunking was at the forefront of my mind. For example, many of the chapters in this book present information in an outline type fashion, such as the subheading "7 goal-setting obstacles." From my experience as a student and simply as a reader, trying to retain and make use of lots of information just becomes overwhelming. Therefore, a primary goal in writing this book is to create a learning tool that is concisely written, providing proven information to help everyone reading this book to, at the very least, give the topic of motivation and its essential ingredients some thought as it relates their lives.

What is this book about?

The essence of this book is about asking yourself and examining the following questions: "What is going on in my life right now?" "Where do I want to be in 3 months, 6 months, a year…5 years, etc.?" "Who do I want to be as I travel the path that is my life?" "What truly motivates me each and every day?"

I like to think the motivational ingredients in this book are analogous to one of my favorite seasonings that I use to enhance the flavor of eggs and chicken. These ingredients are French basil, French tarragon, purple shallots, chives, bay leaves, and dillweed. When combined, these ingredients turn eggs and bland chicken into a very tasty meal, without adding salt. Similarly, when you use the motivational ingredients in this book appropriately, on a *consistent* basis, they will improve the quality of your everyday life. The ingredients for keeping your motivational spirit solid as a rock serve to add "flavor" to your life just as my one of my favorite seasonings adds much-needed flavor to my food.

Chapter **1** is about discovering and becoming aware of the interesting complexities of motivation. In this chapter, some illuminating research-based strategies for building confidence and the correlation between an optimistic mindset and confidence are discussed. Overall, this chapter presents you with the multifaceted nature of motivation. Chapter **2,** Motivation in Action, tells the story of an innovative doctor whose motivation propelled him to embark on a unique business idea. This chapter also presents 3 hypothetical case studies, designed to illustrate how these motivational ingredients are put to constructive use. Chapter **3** on goal setting is designed to do exactly what the title of the chapter suggests: keep you on track with a vision of success! Two of the many topics covered in this chapter are understanding the goal creation process using your M.A.P.S acronym, and the basic framework for implementing an effective goal setting program. The essence of Chapter **4** is about having a clear understanding of what, why, when, where, and how you need to accomplish your goals. This is a short chapter, but profoundly important because without effective communication, achieving your goals and dreams are compromised by misunderstandings, uncertainty, and doubt. Effective communication greatly improves motivation by fostering positive, respectful relationships, and team cohesion. Such topics as the three primary characteristics of effective communication and the major factors affecting effective communication are discussed in this chapter. Chapter **5** presents lots of research-based evidence proving that stress and anxiety truly are barriers to achieving your goals and realizing your dreams. This chapter also provides a hypothetical case study of Cheryl, who is having difficulty navigating her way through the rehabilitation process.

Chapter **6** provides you with the necessary tools to regulate your motivation by covering such topics as the 5 contributing factors to over-arousal. Chapter **7** examines what it truly means to "zero in on your goals," by understanding distractions and gaining an awareness of the 4 general types of focusing styles, learning them, and practicing them. This chapter also explores the concept of centering and how it can benefit you when you need to hit the "reset button." Chapter **8** is about your self-dialogue, which has the potential to greatly impact your actions, and chances for success and happiness. Chapter **9** showcases exactly why *positive thinking* is the foundation of motivation. The fact is, without a positive mindset it is nearly impossible to see positive possibilities because your ability to focus in a goal-directed fashion is compromised by the "dark clouds" of negativity. Such concepts as the relationship between mood, memory, and positive thinking are examined in this foundational chapter. Chapter **10** is about imagining yourself accomplishing your goals and achieving the success that you seek through the use of imagery practice. Two of the topics discussed are the 5 characteristics of successful imagery practice and research-based benefits of consistent imagery practice. The goal of Chapter **11** is to ask you to reflect on the importance of time as it pertains to your goals, life plans, and motivation. I share some memorable experiences in this chapter and connect it with an important concept discussed in the book.

Why did I write this book?

The primary reason that I wrote this book is rooted in my belief that as human beings, at our core, motivation is designed to create a life purpose and a sense of meaning. Since the "genesis of my motivational spirit" I have had two foundational goals to accomplish with my life: help others in any way that I can and lead a life path that is healthy, productive, and meaningful. Although, I did not go on to compete in bodybuilding contests extensively throughout the course of my life, competing and training set the stage for my life in terms of fueling my motivational spirit. Competing in bodybuilding competitions taught me that goal accomplishment is *transferable*, in that, quite often, when we accomplish a goal in one area, such as graduating college, winning a contest, etc., confidence is then boosted, subsequently facilitating a belief in accomplishing another challenging goal.

A secondary reason for writing this book resides in my ability to reach down and exhibit some resiliency. Unfortunately, due to genetics and overuse, repetitive pattern overload, I developed some lower back issues/pain during the past 4-5 years. You may be wondering, how does this happen to someone with an extensive personal training and health coaching background? The short answer is, a considerable amount of damage had already been done to my lower back by the time I acquired the knowledge I have now, particularly pertaining to stretching muscles after overuse. I owned a small cleaning business for a number of years that entailed a great deal of twisting and bending, which contributed a considerable amount to the problem. During the past eight months, I have been "sidelined" from doing the things that my motivational spirit drives me to do. However, navigating my way through the rehabilitation process has allowed me to truly make use of the tools in this book and place my focus in a goal-directed fashion, hence writing this book. I wrote this book for all of us who are facing obstacles that at times test the strength of our motivational spirit.

I have found through the writing of this book, the more I go over the material and learn it, the end result is that the words increase in value, acquiring more meaning and depth, because such skills as the ability to adequately focus, when, where, how, and on what is essential to everyday life, whether you are a high school basketball player or someone who works in your company's human resource department.

The core goal of this book is to provide the essential ingredients to keep your motivational spirit solid as a rock! It is my hope that you find this book to be informative and insightful, thus creating awareness... which is the "door" to goals and dreams being realized!

Robert

Chapter 1

Motivation:
The Fuel that Drives us Toward our Goals

"Motivation will almost always beat mere talent." —*Norman R. Augustine*

What Is Motivation?

The topic of motivation is a multifaceted one. In short, it's an "intangible variable that ebbs and flows widely in short periods of time."[1] Athletes with seemingly unparalleled drive lose it. Some people show up to practice one day with a fire lit inside them, and the next day, the motivational fire has fizzled out. From week to week, teams, athletes, coaches, and workers fluctuate in their intensity and level of dedication.

Motivation is the tendency to pursue, engage, and persist in activities related to your chosen interest and goals. In essence, it is the direction and intensity of the effort you put forth to successfully complete a given task. Direction indicates *what* you pursue, and the intensity is *how much* effort you put forth. For example, you could make a choice to attend practice over a social event (your direction suggests that you are motivated); however, you proceed to kid around with teammates throughout practice (your level of intensity suggests a lack of motivation).

Direction indicates *what* activity is pursued. For instance, Lucy the basset hound is pursuing one of her favorite pastimes, napping.

In the next picture, we see a group of athletes in pursuit of the finish line. The other component of motivation, intensity, is about how much effort is being exerted toward the activity being pursued. In both pictures, maximum effort is being exerted toward reaching a desired goal. In the picture above, the desired outcome is sleep, whereas in the next picture, the goal is winning the race or setting a personal best record.

It is essential to look at both aspects (direction and intensity) in efforts to better understand motivation, but it is equally as important to note that motivation is a complex concept and that motivation will vary from individual to individual, and also across situations from one individual to the next.

The word **motivation** is derived from the Latin word "movere," meaning "to move," and describes the often powerful inner voice that activates you to direct your behavior in a specific fashion.[2] Synonyms include "desire," "get-up-and-go," "zip," and "oomph." Whatever you choose to call it, motivation is clearly a key component of performance; without it, you are never fully psychologically ready to compete or complete the task at hand.

Its influence is essential to your daily life. A complete absence of motivation equals inertia, no activity at all. This is an unnatural state for human beings because we all possess a deep-seated need to explore and master our environment to help our own survival. Thus, nobody is completely devoid of motivation. What individuals sometime need to discover is the key that unlocks their own motivational spirit. Your motivational spirit is the fuel that will fulfill your potential.

The Most Basic Motivation: Survival of One's Species:
Considering motivation is about the direction and intensity goals are pursued, the coho salmon and the leatherback turtle are interesting and great examples of what can be accomplished with this inner drive shared by all species, called motivation.

The coho salmon has an amazing life journey that is guided by one goal, which is to survive in order to reproduce. Some salmon swim more than 1,000 miles depending upon where they live, having obstacles to overcome along the way such as dams, waterfalls, upstream currents, and predators to reach their freshwater breeding grounds. The leatherback turtle also is very impressive with its continuous series of transoceanic migrations to reproduce and find food. For example, researchers tracked the journey of a turtle that began on an Indonesian beach, where this leatherback turtle laid the last of her eggs. Then her motivation to complete the task at hand, propelled her to crawl to the water, and begin her tremendous voyage consisting of 12,774 miles, ending off the coast of Oregon; it is here where the leather back turtle feeds. Like all goal pursuits, outcome goals are accomplished through consistent daily goals, fueled by motivation. Here we have the leatherback turtle, a rather large marine reptile migrating approximately 20 miles per day for 647 days! This incredibly impressive long-term goal accomplishment by the leatherback turtle was tracked by a radio beacon attached to her back, and was actually one of the longest such migrations by any vertebrate animal.[3]

A clear understanding of *how* motivation is activated is valuable. At any given moment, you are faced with a dilemma, given that life, with its endless variety, offers an immense range of activities that compete for your time. If offered a choice, some individuals would exercise or play a sport, some would lie on the coach eating a large bowl of chocolate and vanilla ice cream and watching TV, and some would choose to read a good book. One person might tire of a chosen activity quickly and decide to stop, whereas another may continue much longer.

You are not a neutral observer of the surrounding world. Some parts of it appeal to you, drive you forward, and make you feel good, whereas other parts provoke anxiety or disgust or just simply don't have any meaning for you. The kind of things, activities, individuals, and environments you like or dislike are bound up with your motivations.

Your motives are very important because they direct your behavior and the life you live; however, everyone does not share the same interest or values. In the same situation, some individuals choose a path that leads in one direction, and others take the opposite route. Individual motivation not only makes our lives different, but it also helps us to select life paths, contexts, and settings that satisfy our individual needs according to our earlier experiences, personal characteristics, and values. Motivation is, therefore, a major concept that helps us to understand why some individuals succeed in living a happy and fulfilling life, while others do not.

Motivation is not only a personal characteristic but also a relationship between your needs and values and the environments that satisfy them. People differ not only in what they find pleasing or what they value but also in their life situations, which provide them with possibilities for satisfying their needs and accomplishing their goals. Being able to create a fulfilling life or a positive development path is not so much about the kinds of life motives you possess or the kind of situation in which you live but rather how you are able to combine these together in a positive manner.

Individual motivation differs according to several personality factors, such as learning history and personality traits. In turn, a person's life and associated constraints, as well as opportunities, are influenced by other factors such as cultural beliefs and values, the demands of a certain life stage, norms, gender roles, society, and historical time. As both individual characteristics and life situations differ significantly, it is easy to see that there are a variety of routes to positive development, just as there are many avenues to negative developmental paths.

Key Point:

Your level of motivation and the personal goals that help you to adapt to your situation(s) in ways that satisfy your individual needs are a major source of your degree of happiness experienced in your daily life.

Specific Age Phase Differences in Human Motivation

Individual's goals vary, and these differences reflect the developmental tasks, opportunities, and role transitions characteristic of a specific age phase. For example, when youths and young adults are asked about their future interest, they usually report goals that reference education, future family, leisure activities, occupation, and self-related subjects. When individuals transition from early to middle adulthood, there are obvious changes in personal goals. For example, Nurmi (1992) discovered that, "while 25-to-34-year-olds often mention goals concerning family and self, 35-to-44-year-olds reported goals related to their children's lives and travel; 45-to-54-year-olds mentioned goals concerning health, children's lives, and leisure activities; and 55-to-64-year-olds had many goals concerning health, leisure activities, and world politics. All age groups reported many occupation- and property-related goals.[4] Cross and Markus (1991), for example, found that elderly people particularly mentioned health- and lifestyle-related topics.[5] Similarly, Smith and Freund (2002)[6] found that very old people's goals are often focused on personal characteristics, health, and social relationships." [7]

Individuals who think that their goals are aligned with their inherent needs report a high level of happiness. Likewise, people who cite that they are committed to achieving their goals, who believe that they can control their goals, and who acknowledge that their goals have advanced well also show a higher degree of happiness. In other words, being optimistic about your chances of attaining your goals that originate out of your internal needs provides a foundation for happiness. Goals assist you in dealing with the demands and opportunities of a certain life period in which you are living. [7] However, excessive self-focus is problematic, perhaps because it leads to ruminative thinking. Although we all need to think about ourselves and evaluate our potential for changing ourselves in positive ways, continuous self-focus tends to lead to a low sense of well-being.

An Essential Function of Motivation

It is important to remember; a key function of motivation is to adjust one's personal goals in ways that improve one's *possibilities* to manage one's current life situation. Individuals who have difficulties in making this adjustment are incapable or unwilling to change their previous goals are at greater risk of feeling unhappy. Additionally, feelings of well-being and happiness are likely to influence the types of goals that individuals create.

A high level of happiness can be assumed to increase focus on interpersonal goals, as well as one's belief in personal control and goal fulfillment. In other words, happiness is likely to lead to the creation of goals that will subsequently contribute to positive feelings about yourself and your life, thus establishing a foundation for a positive life trajectory.

What Are Attributions and the 3 Critical Elements You Need to Know About?

Attributions are simply explanations for things that occur in our lives. If you win a crucial match for your school's tennis team, to what do you **attribute** your success? Perhaps your new practice schedule is beginning to pay off? Maybe your opponent was playing with a minor injury? Did you have the benefit of home court advantage?

Individuals regularly make attributions in an attempt to make sense out of their experiences. These attributions encompass inferences that eventually represent guesswork on each person's behalf.

Fritz Heider (1958) [8] was the first to state that individuals tend to locate the cause of behavior either within a person, attributing it to personal variables, or outside of an individual, assigning it to environmental and situational factors. He accordingly established 1 of the 3 critical dimensions along which attributions are made: internal or external, the two other dimensions are controllable-uncontrollable and stable-unstable. [9]

A Closer Look at Attributions

1) Internal or External

Expanding on Heider's insight, numerous theorists have argued that explanations of behavior and events can be *categorized* as internal or external attributions. Internal attributions assign the causes of behavior to abilities, personal dispositions, traits, and feelings. External attributions assign the causes of behavior to environmental constraints and situational demands. [9] For example, if you attribute your poor math grade to your inability to prepare sufficiently for the test (low motivation) or to getting excessively anxious during the test, you are making internal attributions. An external attribution may be that the course is simply too difficult, not of real interest to you, or that the math book is incomprehensible.

2) Stable or Unstable

A second dimension individuals utilize in making casual attributions is the stability of the cause underlying a given behavior. A stable cause is one that is more or less permanent and doubtful to change over time. For example, intelligence and a sense of humor are *stable internal* causes of behavior. *Stable external* causes of behavior involve such things as laws and rules (no smoking area, speed limits, etc.,). Unstable causes of behavior are subject to change. *Unstable internal* causes of behavior involve such things as motivation (strong or weak) and mood (good or bad). The presence or absence of other people and weather conditions are very good examples of *unstable external* causes of behavior. [9]

3) Controllable or Uncontrollable

This dimension in the attribution process recognizes the fact that sometimes events are under your control and sometimes they are not. For instance, the amount of effort you spend on a task is usually viewed as something under your control, whereas a talent for music is perceived as something you are born with (beyond your control). [9]

These three dimensions are the fundamental ones in the attribution process. Research has shown that self-attributions are motivational, guiding us toward or away from conceivable courses of action. Therefore, your self-beliefs can greatly influence future expectations (success or failure) as well as emotions (guilt, hopelessness, pride), and these expectations and emotions have the potential to combine to impact subsequent behavior and performances. Self-attributions, thus, play a vital role in your feelings, behaviors, and motivational state. [9]

Self-Determination Theory

Self-Determination Theory states that whether or not an individual has more or less self-determined reasons for participating in their chosen physical activity is dependent on his or her degree of basic need satisfaction. Athletes and non-athletes alike need to feel self-directed, competent, and connected. When your environment meets these 3 basic needs, there will be a greater degree of self-determination, investment, as well as happiness in a given setting, thus contributing to a motivational climate that fosters growth and goal attainment. Importantly noted, if one or more of these needs are not satisfied, poor functioning and performances are often the result. [10]

The Impact of Competence, Control, and Relatedness on Motivation

Competence, control, and relatedness have the ability to enhance or drastically increase motivation. For example, if an athlete is in a situation where they feel they are competent (believe that they can handle the task), if they feel they have some control or say in what goes on, and if they feel connected to others around them, then motivation will be enhanced. The opposite is true as well. If you feel like you are lacking competence or that the environment/situation suggests that you are not able to handle the tasks that you are supposed to, if you have no control and choice in your activity/sport life, etc., or if you are feeling a lack of relatedness to the others in your environment, then your motivation will decrease.[10]

Task-Mastery vs. Ego-Oriented Orientations

People with a *task-mastery orientation* are those who take pride in improvement of their own skill and knowledge and concentrate on their ability relative to their own past performances. For example, a cross-country runner who judges his success according to his personal record is task-oriented, while a basketball player who judges his or her success compared to other players in the game may be said to be *ego-oriented.*; this refers to the tendency of an individual to concentrate on social comparisons. Ego-orientated athletes are motivated by the desire to demonstrate superiority over other competitors. [10]

Task orientation is associated with the *process* of improvement, while ego orientation focuses on the *outcome* of a competition or event. It is essential to understand the impact of these orientations, and perhaps create more of a balance if you tend to be highly ego-oriented. [10]

Intrinsic vs. Extrinsic Motivation

When participation in a physical activity is inherently pleasurable, when the direction and intensity of effort is based on enjoyment, excitement, and the desire to improve, an individual is said to have intrinsic motivation. When participation is about acquiring rewards, trophies, a higher salary, a scholarship, for example, the individual is said to have extrinsic motivation. [10]

An Example of Intrinsic Motivation

1996 Wimbledon Semifinals:

At Wimbledon in July 1996, Steffi Graf reached the semifinals, Graf had a chance to win for the seventh time in the Wimbledon women's singles championship. A win would have brought her into second place behind Margaret Court, who achieved twenty-four grand slam titles. Graf pointed out that:

"I am happy if I win the match and happier if I play well. That's more important to me than records. Maybe at the end of my career that's something I can look back on and be proud of, but not right now." [11]

Strategies for Providing a Solid Foundation for Increasing Intrinsic Motivation

Positive Self-Dialogue/Seeking the Positives in Life, Mission Statements, Goal Setting, A Vision for Success, Improving Weakness in your Chosen Sport, and Varying Training/Exercise Routines

Motivational Insight

Confidence and motivation have a direct correlation (relationship, not causation); this is supported by research. The most significant determinant influencing confidence is *past performance.* Other important factors that influence this relationship include: emotional states, vicarious experiences, imaginal experiences, and physiological states. [10]

Defining Confidence

Confidence is the absolute belief that you have the necessary knowledge, skills, and abilities to successfully complete a particular task or goal. Confidence is *both* a trait (a stable component of personality) and a state (how you feel at any given moment). Thus, confidence is considered a part of personality. Some individuals will always possess more confidence than others by nature. Fluctuations in a person's confidence are dictated by circumstances and their reactions to those situations. [2] However, it is this variation of confidence that you can learn to control by staying connected to your motivational spirit!

Prerequisites for Gaining Confidence

Possessing an understanding of the interaction of thoughts and behavior/performance, creating and maintaining self-awareness, possessing a positive mind-set, and embracing an attitude of excellence

5 Benefits of Being Confident

1) Confidence increases effort.

The amount of effort you expend and how long you will persist in pursuit of a goal depends largely on your level of confidence.

2) Confidence impacts goal selection.

Confident individuals set challenging goals and pursue them with full effort.

3) Confidence impacts psychological momentum.

Possessing the ability to produce positive momentum or reverse negative momentum is a significant asset; confidence is a key ingredient in this process. Individuals who are confident in themselves and their abilities have a "never give up," attitude. They perceive situations that seem as obstacles as an opportunity for a challenge, responding with increased determination.

4) Confidence produces positive emotions.

When you feel confident, you are much more likely to remain calm under pressure.

5) Confidence increases your ability to focus.

When you feel confident, your mind is in a positive state, free to focus on the task at hand.

Illuminating Research-Based Strategies for Building Confidence

According to Professors Albert Bandura and Deborah Feltz, there are several effective ways in which you can increase your level of confidence. The following are arranged in order of efficiency: performance achievements, indirect experience (involves experiencing success through a teammate, friend or family member), verbal persuasion (is derived from yourself, significant others, coaches, teammates, and role models), and control of physiological states (prevents unnecessary bodily stress from inhibiting performance). [2]

The Correlation between Having an Optimistic Mindset and Confidence

Developing an optimistic mindset maximizes the influence of attributions on confidence. The first key to creating an optimistic mindset is to seek positive feedback. You must learn to turn up the volume on positive sources and to hit the silence button on the negative sources. A good analogy for the optimistic individual is one possessing "rose-tinted glasses." Put special focus on the word *tinted* here because having "rose-*colored* glasses" may present the tendency for us to lose objectivity in various situations. Possessing an optimistic mindset allows us to see new possibilities for improvement and growth, subsequently staying connected to our motivational spirit.

In an ideal world, confidence should remain stable across a variety of circumstances. A confident football player, for example, will accept the bad result without the unnecessary self-blame. "Legendary American football coach Vince Lombardi once explained that confidence when you are winning isn't real confidence. Everyone is confident when they are winning. Real confidence occurs when athletes are losing but are still able to maintain self-belief, or when they learn from their failures and move on." [2]

The Optimistic Mindset in Action

"I've missed more than 9,000 shots in my career. I've lost almost 300 games. Twenty-six times I've been trusted to take the game winning shot and missed. I've failed over and over and over again in my life. And that is why I succeed." —Michael Jordan [2]

To Create or Restore your Confidence

First identify the factor (s) that are responsible for the decrease in your confidence level. *Second*, establish images of confidence along with the specific nature of your "winning feeling." *Third*, perform an imagery exercise to fully experience the desired confident state. *Fourth*, create goals to turn obstacles into positive challenges and opportunities for growth. *Lastly*, and most importantly, a feeling of personal control over events is the foundation of confidence. You can facilitate this by accomplishing a series of small tasks (confidence builders), which collectively assist you in overcoming any major barriers in pursuit of reaching your desired confidence level.

Your motivation is the fuel for the journey of change and goal achievement, it will get you through inevitable and unpredictable setbacks, moments of doubt and any other things that arises to potentially throw you off course. The question to ask is: "Is there something in your life that's important to you that's being impacted by your relative inability to focus the way you want and need to, and/or is your sense of being overwhelmed by the vast number of stimuli and messages competing for your attention?"

Remember

The best source of motivation is to connect the change you seek to a *higher purpose*, one of great meaning to you, assessing how will it help you do the things that make you thrive, thus realizing your life's purpose, and or make a positive difference in the world.

Creating a Source of Motivation through a Mission Statement

A mission statement represents the essence of *why* you want to pursue and accomplish specific goals. A mission statement can enhance motivation because the statement itself and the exercise of creating one assist you in remembering and identifying the motivation that you possess for your chosen pursuits. Creating a mission statement involves 4 key steps:

Step 1: Ask yourself, "What motivates me to pursue this goal? What do I ultimately *expect* to achieve from fulfilling this goal?"

Step 2: Use all of your motivating factors, feelings, people, images, to specify a purpose and a mission. As a "rule of thumb," narrow down the list before trying to create a mission statement; otherwise, the next step of the process will most likely become overwhelming.

Step 3: Having narrowed down some of the strongest factors, combine these motivating ingredients into a single written statement.

Step 4: Use the mission statement, put it in key places, such as on your refrigerator, locker or gym bag. Whether you are creating a mission statement for yourself or with a team, one of the most significant aspects of this exercise is that you write down the mission statement and post it where it can be seen, by those who need to see it.

Closing Thought

Resiliency is an essential aspect of motivation because it is the ability to bounce back successfully after exposure to severe risk, stress or injury; in essence, it is righting of oneself in conditions that has created some additional challenges. The central point here is that challenges and setbacks inevitably occur to all of us; thus, being resilient is key to staying connected to your motivational spirit!

Chapter 2

Motivation in Action:
Great Examples Designed to Inspire and Empower

The 2nd longest Tennis Match in Australian Open History[1]

Rafael Nadal played against Fernando Verdasco in the 2009 Australian Open semifinals. Nadal somehow managed to stay in the game, as Verdasco was hitting a very high percentage of outright winning shots. After five hours and fourteen minutes of intense back-and-forth play, Nadal won in five sets. During the match it was so hot that both players utilized ice packs around their necks and shoulders between games. After this marathon of a match, Nadal's legs could barely carry him. The match with Verdasco had taken a toll on Nadal physically; this was a concern, considering he needed to start preparing for his match against Roger Federer.

Fortunately, Nadal had an excellent support team, some of which had been with him since he was nine or ten years old, coaching and supporting his career as a tennis player. Nadal's support team was very optimistic, highlighting the fact that their pre-season training had been preparing them for just such an occasion. They all agreed that the most important thing on Nadel's recovery agenda was to get his body moving, back in action, getting his blood flowing, staying motivated.

Typically, the day before a final, Nadal trained in the morning. However, this time he slept all morning, waking up in the afternoon to discover, horrified, that he felt stiffer than the night before. The next course of action entailed pedaling away on a stationary bike, in efforts to just get the blood circulating, and then he went on the court to practice; this lasted barely twenty minutes. It was obvious that Nadal could not continue, he was so stiff that he could barely move. Although Nadal's support team, and coaching staff were working overtime to get him ready for the next day's final, in that moment, his confidence was slipping away, disconnecting from his motivational spirit.

He went to sleep that night in a bad mood and woke up the next morning feeling a little less stiff. However, with a mere two and a half hours before the start of the match, he was still experiencing leg cramps, resulting in a feeling of dizziness. Nadal's uncle, Toni, also a member of his coaching staff, was there, and after half an hour struggling to get a rhythm going, it was concluded, once again, that Nadal could not continue; he really felt and looked terrible. Nadal went back to the locker room, and this is when his uncle Toni, rose to the occasion. His uncle's strength comes from the power of his words, which connected with Nadal's motivational spirit. Toni reminded Nadal that the most valuable training they did when he was a kid was not on the court but instead during the discussions they had in the car going to and from tennis matches. They would plan ahead of time what they would do or evaluate afterward what went right and what went wrong. This is a point I emphasize throughout this book: planning and preparedness greatly assist in overcoming challenges!

Toni tells Nadal, "Look, it's five-thirty now, and when you go on court at seven-thirty I assure you, you won't be feeling any better. You'll probably be feeling worse. So, it's up to you whether you rise above the pain and the exhaustion and summon up the desire you need to win. Don't say you can't. Because anybody who digs deep enough can always find motivation they need for anything. Just imagine if there were a guy sitting behind you in the stadium pointing a gun at you, telling you that if you didn't run, and keep running, he'd shoot you. I bet you'd run then. So, come on! It's up to you to find the motivation to win. Even if there's only a one percent chance of you winning this match, well, then, you have to squeeze every last drop out of that one percent." [1]

Nadal listened attentively to his Uncle Toni's inspiring words; his goal would be to focus less on his aches and pains and more about creating a plan. His coaching staff stressed the need to play the match "ergonomically," which meant he needed to adjust his game to the realities of the physical condition he was in. This meant Nadal needed more pacing than he typically did, thus saving his body's reserves of energy for the more crucial points and not putting full effort into every single point as if it were his last.

Armed with a game plan Nadal took his usual cold shower, after which he did feel better, and performed his sequence of pre-match rituals in the locker room with a sense of growing belief. When he went out on court, he wasn't hobbling anymore. The aches were still present, and he felt a little slow during the warm-up with Federer. Sure enough, his left foot, the tarsal scaphoid bone, started bothering him again. But he reminded himself that he been there before and hoped that the adrenaline and his ability to focus would triumph over the pain one more time. He regained his confidence by believing that he could rise to the occasion. At that moment, the challenging task of overcoming the predicament he was in became something not of fear but rather something to relish!

Once the match began, Nadal's pain diminished—so much so that he was able to fully focus, thus allowing him to win the first game. As the games went on, he found out, to his great relief, that he wasn't panting and out of breath. Nadal reminded himself that pain resides in the mind. If you can *control* your mind, you can, therefore, control your body. He lost the fourth set, just as he had done against Fernando Verdasco, after having gone up two sets to one, but he came back, his determination bolstered and his motivational spirit enhanced by the surprise and enjoyment he felt at having made it as far as he did without falling apart. Uncle Toni had been right. Nadal could win, and he did win the 2009 Australian Open Championship, beating Roger Federer in five sets!

Rafael Nadal's lesson from this experience was one that his Uncle Toni had been strongly emphasizing for many years, which was that you always have to hang in there, persevere through the tough times, and view obstacles as challenges, however remote the chances of winning seem. You have to believe in yourself and push yourself to the very limits of your abilities; this is truly a great example of resiliency!

Natalie's Story: [2]

Natalie du Toit had dreamed of participating in the Olympics since she was six years old. Natalie set numerous records as a young swimmer, in addition to competing in her first international race at age 14. Her career was going in the same direction of her Olympic dream, and at age 16 she came very close when she nearly qualified for three events leading up to the 2000 Sydney Olympics. She was without a doubt one of the most promising athletes in South Africa; it was simply a matter of time before she accomplished her goals and realized her dream.

In February of 2001, Natalie had a morning that began like any other morning. She had just completed her workout and was driving away on her scooter going to school. As she rode down the street from the pool, she was struck by a car, and in that moment Natalie's life was changed forever. The accident was so devastating that it resulted in the amputation of her left leg, right above the knee. When Natalie talks about her experience, her motivational spirit shines bright: "I have always had a dream to take part in an Olympic Games, and losing my leg didn't change anything." [2] Upon hearing Natalie's story our initial thoughts very well may be that of lost hopes and dreams, but not for Natalie—her willpower was unstoppable. As soon as her surgery was finished, all her thoughts where focused on getting back in the pool. Three years after her accident happened, she went to Athens and won five gold medals competing in the 2004 Paralympic Games.

Natalie's aspirations and goals did not stop there. In 2008, she became one of the most inspiring and motivational stories of the summer. She shocked the world and made history by qualifying for the Olympics and Paralympics that year. During the 2008 Beijing Olympics, Natalie carried the flag for South Korea during the opening ceremonies, with tears in her eyes. She went on to finish 16th in the 10k open water swim with a time of two hours and 49.9 seconds. She also added another five gold medals from the 2008 Paralympics to match her 2004 Paralympics accomplishment. [2] During the 2012 Paralympic Games in London she won three gold medals and narrowly missed out on winning a fourth gold medal during the final race of her impressive career. She never had a goal of becoming an inspirational athlete. Natalie wasn't out to prove anything; she just kept moving forward, staying focused on her goals. "Even when bad things happen you have to try to use those bad things in a positive manner and really just take the positive out of it." [2] Natalie's story is without a doubt impressive, resiliency at its best, for sure. However, it is also a testament to the foundation of motivation: positive thinking!

A Doctor's Innovative Vision [3]

Dr. Jason McMillan, owner of *Mint Dental Works*, located in Portland, Oregon, was motivated to start his venture in efforts to build an earth-friendly office. His goal was to create a space that was different than most people's perception of what a dental office is. In dentistry there are a lot of smells that patients associate with medical or dental procedures. With this in mind, he wanted to tackle the problem that most people associate with going to the dentist, which is simply that of an unpleasant experience, due in large part to the "sterile medical environment" seen in most dental offices.

Dr. Jason McMillan developed his solution to the unpleasant experience that many people feel when going to the dentist by utilizing the LEED umbrella. This gave him a solid framework to build the healthiest environment for his patients, staff, and himself. LEED, or Leadership in Energy and Environmental Design, is responsible for changing the way we think about how buildings and communities are planned, constructed, maintained and operated. Leaders around the world have made LEED the most widely utilized third-party verification for green buildings, with approximately 1.85 million square feet being certified on a daily basis. LEED-certified buildings are resource efficient; they use less water and energy, as well as reduce greenhouse gas emissions. Additionally, as an added bonus, they save money.

Mint Dental Works are addressing their problem and achieving their goals by looking at what's the best way that they can build a highly functional office, while being mindful of materials that are utilized and how the space reflects their ideas and what they're doing in the space, which is providing healthcare. In a traditional evacuation system, which is an important part of a dental office; they use water to drive an impeller that creates suction, and during that process it's taking perfectly clean water and flushing it down the drain. In order to create a more efficient indoor air quality system, a drive evacuation system was incorporated; this system *does not* use water; therefore, in this one piece of equipment, a few hundred thousand gallons of water a year are saved! All of the adhesives, all of the paints, the carpets, the flooring materials are low VOC, therefore limiting the amount of off-gassing that you get in a traditional space.

Dr. Jason McMillan's innovative vision of creating an earth-friendly dental office in a manner in which he was able to accomplish this task was quite impressive. He created a space that was more inviting; that didn't have a sterile, claustrophobic feel to it; and the LEED process really encouraged using reclaimed recycled materials. He discovered the exciting prospect of being able to incorporate salvage was interesting just from a creative perspective; it gave him an opportunity to do something that you wouldn't normally expect to see in a dental office. For example, a lot of the accessory pieces were found objects, such as an old egg incubator. Doors were all reclaimed, coming out of the Portland Hotel, a table that is an old bowling alley floor from just down the street, and an industrial sewing machine stand. These elements add unique earth-friendly character to Mint Dental Works.

Case Study Examples

Case Study 1: *Frank*

Frank is a junior in college, attending on a diving scholarship. He has a history of being a very strong competitor who pushes himself to excel. Quite often this has equaled competitive success; Frank has won a lot, and sometimes easily, at every level of competition.

Frank has decided to start working with me at the request of his coach, who has been witnessing a change in Frank's attitude. Coach McMillian tells me about some of what he has been seeing: "Basically, Frank isn't smiling and laughing with his fellow teammates very much, he seems a bit sluggish in practice, and has been easily distracted." Frank informs me that school has gotten much harder, (he is studying to become a doctor), and he has a new girlfriend (Molly). He still loves diving; however, he isn't enjoying it as much, and he is annoyed with himself because he hasn't been placing higher in recent diving competitions. He used to get "fired up" for competing; the adrenaline would hit him quickly, with ease, without him having to even think about it, and he greatly misses and needs to recapture that feeling.

Frank is interested in trying some strategies that I believe will help him turn his current challenges into an opportunity to reconnect with his motivational spirit. He wants to feel the excitement and enjoyment again for his chosen sport, and definitely has a goal of diving competitively through his senior year.

Addressing Frank's Motivational Concerns:

First, I explain to Frank that motivation is essentially what drives individuals to do what they do. Special emphasis is placed on the significance of understanding Frank's motivation, in order to best address his needs. Considering that an athlete's ability to sustain motivation is highly dependent on a concept called "goal orientation," he is exhibiting difficulty maintaining his motivation as seen by his sluggish play in practice. I describe to Frank the two types of goal orientation that comprise a person's motives (task-mastery vs. ego-oriented). The objective here is to find out if he is task-oriented or goal-oriented because it is important to assist him to understand the impact of these 2 types of goal orientations, and possibly create more of a balance if he tends to be highly ego-oriented.

Second, I address how Frank attributes his performances in sport. What does he perceive to be the explanation(s) for the events currently unfolding in his life? We would want to explore the following: causality of his attributions: internal or external, stability as it relates to his perception that the same outcome will happen again, and how much *control* he perceives he has over the outcome. I provide Frank with a vital piece of information, which is that typically internal, stable, and controllable success attributions are preferable for enhancing motivation.

Frank mentions that school has gotten much harder, and diving hasn't been as enjoyable recently, and he is upset that he hasn't been placing higher in recent diving competitions. Frank's comments lead me to my *third* point; I explain to Frank that the "motivational climate," in which he is currently living is also having an impact on his motivation. Frank needs to understand that if the motivational climate is different than his goal orientation, then his interest and motivation will decline as a result.

Frank has not been smiling and laughing with teammates very much. I explain to him the importance of competence, control, and relatedness, and how they have the ability to increase intrinsic motivation and team cohesion.

Strategies to Assist Frank Regain His Excitement and Enthusiasm for Diving:

I utilize the following strategies in assisting Frank regain his enthusiasm and excitement for diving. First, I ask Frank why he participates in sports. What makes him passionate about playing? What are all the qualities that he likes about his sport? What does he *feel* like when he is motivated? I suggest a few examples of "energy words" that may come to mind, such as agile, focused, ready, strong, powerful, etc.

I explain to Frank that a really good way to explore these questions is to create a mission statement because a mission statement can revitalize his motivational spirit. Creating a mission statement, which is Frank's reason(s) for participating in his chosen sport, will help Frank recall and identify the *core motivators* that he possesses for his sport. I emphasize that an important aspect of this exercise is to *write down* the mission statement and post it where it can be reflected upon, every day, thus making it a positive habit.

I recommend to Frank that he utilize the "energy words" that he thought of when he formulated his mission statement, in order to regain some enthusiasm. In connection with using verbal cues, energizing imagery is a great way for Frank to increase his level of motivation. I point out to Frank that energizing imagery is very effective when fatigue is starting to set in. Also, breathing exercises are not only beneficial for relaxing but also useful for energizing. Having Frank increase his breathing rate in times of needed energy will provide another means of increasing motivation.

I work with Frank to establish a goal for him to combine breathing techniques, verbal cues, and imagery during times of low motivation. These strategies are especially useful because he can use these during practice and during the midst of an important diving performance.

Additional suggestions for Frank include: utilizing positive self-dialogue, varying training, using music for needed energy; getting plenty of rest, maintaining a healthy diet, and keeping his goals at the forefront of his mind. Frank should let his dreams create a vision that beckons him toward his goals. My last suggestion for Frank is to always set goals that are specific and attainable.

Case Study 2: *Pamala*

Pamala is a junior in high school and plays on the school's tennis team. She is hoping to acquire a scholarship to play tennis at her hometown college.

Pamala has very effective ground strokes and tends to be a baseline player. Recently, in practices and in matches, she has been over-hitting her forehand. She attempts to slow it down and ends up becoming increasingly frustrated, over-hitting even more. Reflecting upon her last few matches she says, "I can't keep the ball in the court, no matter what I try. My arm seems to tense up a lot...I just don't know." Pamala's forehand has been disappointing her so much that she feels hesitant and nervous about using it. She has been permitting her frustration to make her hurry her entire game. When she rushes, her breathing becomes shallow, and then she has considerable difficulty recovering between points. She has lost her last 4 matches and is worried about losing her #2 spot on the team. Pamala is also having difficulty sleeping the night before matches because of uncertainties surrounding her chances for a scholarship; such uncertainties are creating a stressful situation for her.

Pamala is very motivated to work with me in efforts to "get back to her game." She is willing to try any new strategies I have that can help end this negative cycle that has impeded her progress.

Addressing Pamala's Motivational Concerns

Before actually assisting Pamala with her performance issues, I find it is essential to explain to her how this negative cycle manifests in such sporting situations. For example, Pamala's statement, "I can't keep the ball in the court, no matter what I try," highlights her perceptive appraisal of the demands, resources, and consequences of the situation.

Pamala is experiencing the negative effects of over-arousal. Therefore, I inform her that each athlete must learn their particular pattern of over-activation resulting from anxiety and worry pertaining to their sport performance. In order to avoid excessive tension, athletes must recognize tension, be able to relax, and release the performance inhibiting tension. This awareness will increase Pamala's sensitivity to tension levels and increase her ability to self-regulate varying levels of tension to equal the demands of the performance situation.

Pamala's assessment affects her emotional and physiological responses (heart rate and muscular tension), this in turn affects her sport performance, such as: motor skills, decision-making, perception, retention of learned information, and execution of specific skills, all of which serve to, once again, affect her perceptual appraisal of the situation. Pamala can visualize this cycle as being increasingly performance debilitating. With this awareness and understanding we are a step closer to creating specific performance enhancing techniques.

Specific Breathing Exercises for Pamala to Utilize

I recommend complete breathing, also called a *circle breath*, as a foundational breathing exercise for Pamala to use. As previously noted, the ability to relax establishes the foundation for learning how to perform momentary relaxation; this will be very beneficial to Pamala during her tennis match. Complete breathing should be practiced at home, or in a quiet, peaceful environment, and after a workout because it is easier to relax a muscle when it is fatigued. Upon learning, Pamala is instructed to take 30 to 40 deep breaths per day. Most importantly, I emphasis concentration breathing because it is a great exercise for athletes who are having difficulty with anxiety and distracting thoughts; it is very beneficial during competition. Concentration breathing is an excellent motivational ingredient for Pamala to utilize when she feels the need to hit the "reset button," and zero in on a process focus.

Another Suggestion for Pamala

A quick body scan is very useful when utilized during competition, such as before Pamala serves a tennis ball. In addition, a neck and shoulder check are useful because athletes often carry excessive tension in the shoulders and neck when they are anxious and tense.

Case Study 3: *Ron*

The fall season was off to a great start for the Sunnybrook golf team as far as wins were concerned. At 3-1, with three matches remaining, they were already making a stronger run than most teams. The weakness in their success, however, was that one of the team's five players did not contribute a single score to the winning total in the first four matches.

Coach Kellerman suggests to Ron, the player who had not yet contributed, that he speak with me regarding his current motivational level. Later that day, Coach Kellerman calls me.

"Do you know Ron?" he asked. Before I could answer, he continued. "Well, he has all the skills in every part of his golf game, and a little extra. Ron hits quite well off the tee, plays his irons better than most on the team, has a very strong short game, and has the potential to consistently putt well. The problem is that he's not scoring for the team. Since he isn't scoring for us, the rest of the team feels like they can't count on him. Now, the rest of the team cannot depend on him, which is ironic, considering he has been one of our best golfers. In fact, Ron had some exceptional rounds last year for us, and was a welcomed addition to the Sunnybrook golf team. However, after not scoring for the team in the first tournament of this year, he began avoiding his teammates, which served to lessen any team cohesion that had existed between Ron and his fellow teammates."

Coach Kellerman also informed me that Ron had qualified for the Southern Amateur, as well as the U.S. Amateur competitions. When Ron was in high school, he was the state runner-up once, and a U.S. Junior Amateur qualifier. However, great as he was, he was known to have a few short lapses of focus each round, which added 4 to 6 strokes to his score, preventing him from winning a medal and accomplishing his goals.

The next day, Ron introduced himself. He began telling me that he is a very good golfer and just can't understand why he hasn't been able to score. Ron said, "I have a couple of spots during most rounds where I hit ridiculously stupid shots!" After a short pause, Ron continued, "I don't understand why this is happening…. I get so mad, and I have to work extra hard to get my shot back that I often put too much oomph on the next couple of shots. I also find myself thinking about the score, and thinking about it, realizing how I need to come up with something big…something really big! Then I feel pressured, if I mess up again, well…it gets me really angry…and at this point the odds of my doing well are not very good!"

After my conversation with Ron, I called Coach Kellerman to inquire more about Ron's lapses in focus. Coach Kellerman and I talked for about 15 minutes. He told me how, out of nowhere and without warning, Ron would hit uncharacteristically bad shots that subsequently cost him a stroke or two. Then, for the next two or three shots, Ron will hang his head, not talking to the others, and generally look defeated. Also, he will slam his bag down and aggressively hit his club against the ground when his shots don't go exactly as he planned.

According to the coach, Ron seems to be behaving like a bad storm on the verge of turning into a tornado with his unpredictability! Then all of a sudden, he returns to hitting near-perfect shots, walking with his head up, and talking to his teammates.

Coach Kellerman stated, "I wish Ron could play consistently like he does for most of his round because if he could do that, the team could count on him to take us to the National Championship this year," even though the Sunnybrook golf team is currently ranked 10th in the nation.

Addressing Ron's Motivational Concerns

The presenting problem is that Ron is not helping his team win because he is having short lapses of focus each round that subsequently adds approximately four to six strokes to his score.

Other issues include underlying themes of pressure, possibly coming from several directions. Due to Ron's abundance of prior success, he may be putting pressure on himself to live up to unrealistic expectations, and his lack of production is putting increased pressure on his teammates. This situation produces a motivational climate that is counterproductive to Ron and his fellow teammates.

The coach expresses concern for how the team and Ron are getting along and enjoying the game of golf. Ron is avoiding his teammates; they may be avoiding him as well. Coach Kellerman needs to improve his communication skills, as evidenced by his not waiting for me to answer his question as to whether I knew Ron before going on a rant. Another underlying theme is the "ifs," which adds to the pressure felt by all. The coach thinks that they could contend for a National Championship if Ron "held it together," even though they are currently ranked 10th in the nation. Ron stated, "If I mess up again, odds of doing well are not very good!" Coach Kellerman and Ron are focusing on "ifs," essentially outcome goals; this facilitates pressure and lapses in focus.

Ron needs to explore *why* he was having fun last year and not this year; his goal orientation needs to be examined as well. In efforts to increase his awareness of his negative self-dialogue, the following motivational ingredients are recommended: countering, creating affirmations, developing a positive mindset, consistent imagery practice, and the utilization of relaxation techniques. Additionally, concentration breathing and centering will especially help Ron hit the "reset button" when his focus begins to stray in crucial moments of competitive play.

Closing Thought

Having clear life goals, which are specifically defined, gives you a sense of direction that can help you overcome problems with motivation.

Chapter 3

Goal Setting:
Keeping You on Track with a Vision of Success

"Goals are dreams with deadlines." —*Diana Scharf Hunt*

A goal is simply an objective of attaining a specific standard of proficiency at a given task, typically within a specified time period. From a practical perspective, goals focus on achieving a specified standard—for example, a baseball player increasing his batting average by 12 percentage points.

The reality is that each day we take a step toward reaching goals, remain the same, or take a step back.

3 Goal-Setting Insights

1) Having clear, specifically defined goals gives you a sense of direction that can assist you in overcoming problems with motivation.
2) Through goal setting, you turn intentions and visions of success into actions and reality!
3) The key to having continued success rests upon reevaluating your goals and having realistic expectations.

Achievement

The concept of achievement is based on setting effective goals; fulfilling objectives very often results in a sense of accomplishment. The fact is, you can only achieve one thing at a time; therefore, you should learn to dedicate all your effort to the most immediate goal to get you to your ultimate destination. It may lie only a short distance along the road of a sporting achievement, or it might be a long, ambitious journey to work your way up the corporate ladder. It is essential to stay focused on the present because you cannot change the past, and by doing so you will create a better present and future.

Awareness

Gaining awareness is the *first* fundamental step in goal setting. Goal setting requires awareness because you must first establish your goals, and then make every effort to reach them, then proceed to evaluate performance feedback, and finally adjust the goals as necessary. When you gain more awareness, you make accurate adjustments in your goal pursuits. This ability to adjust the subtle details of performance is a vital skill to have as you pursue your goals.

5 Ways Utilizing Goals Are Important to You

1) Goals direct your attention and effort toward goal-relevant activities and away from goal-irrelevant activities.
2) Goals have an energizing function; high-level goals lead to greater effort than low-level goals.
3) Goals affect persistence. When you control the time you spend on a task, challenging goals prolong effort.
4) Goals influence action indirectly by leading to the discovery and/or use of task-relevant knowledge and strategies.
5) Appropriate goal setting assists in keeping your motivational spirit solid as a rock!

7 Goal-Setting Guidelines

1) Set specific goals in behavioral terms.
2) Set realistic yet challenging goals.
3) Set long-term (3-month) and short-term (weekly and daily) goals.

4) Set positive goals, not negative goals.
5) Establish actual dates for attaining your goals.
6) Create goal achievement strategies—for example, writing them down on paper or posting them on your refrigerator (a place that you will likely see it a few times a day).
7) Find others who support your pursuit of your goals.

5 Types of Goals

1) Outcome Goals **2**) Long-Term Goals **3**) Performance Goals **4**) Weekly Goals **5**) Daily Goals

Five Outcome-Goal Examples

1) Bench-pressing 225 pounds
2) Finishing first in my weight class, bodybuilding competition
3) Winning the NBA Finals
4) Winning the Super Bowl
5) Earning an A in math class

New Year's resolutions are examples of outcome goals (e.g., "I want to lose 20 pounds or get in shape.") Without the behavioral component, especially the necessary action steps, individuals are unlikely to be successful in accomplishing their goals. Breaking down outcome goals into specific steps make success much more likely. Specific *action steps* are analogous to the way we would approach the goal of walking 10 miles, simply one step at a time.

Long-Term Goal Example

Mike is averaging 75% accuracy in free-throw shots. (Time frame: 3 months)

Right now: He is shooting 65% accuracy in free-throw shots.

Mike should combine a verbal cue with an imagery technique (a visual of a smooth release and follow-through), utilize the verbal cue, "focus" prior to shooting free throws, and increase his practice time from 1 day a week to 3 days a week.

5 Performance Goal Examples:

1) Improve consistency of workouts from 2 days a week to 3 days a week.
2) Improve 5k run time from 32 minutes to 30 minutes.
3) Improve batting average from .283 to .300.
4) Improve execution of lunges with dumbbells.
5) Improve execution of top spin in tennis.

5 Weekly Goals Examples

1) Four days this week, I will eat whole wheat toast for breakfast.

2) Bring lunch to work 5 days a week.
3) I will listen to jazz music on vinyl for an hour Friday night to relax and set the tone for a relaxing weekend.
4) I will go to the gym 3 days this week and work out at home twice.
5) I will ride my bike to work 2 times this week, in addition to my planned workouts.

Weekly Goals Represent Consistent Steps to Achieving Your 3-Month Goals:

Weekly goals allow you to take small steps toward your 3-month goals. It is important that you step out of your comfort zone each week to experience the increased sense of confidence that comes from effectively going beyond your perceived limits. I recommend, setting goals that you can reach at least 60% (preferably 70%) of the time because if goal success is less than 60%, the goals are quite likely too ambitious.

Set Specific Daily Goals:

You need to know with certainty what you want to achieve every day. Make a commitment to yourself to execute your skills with 100% focus. Importantly noted, positive imagery can benefit you in preparing your mind and body to perform at your best. Perhaps a good idea for some people may be to practice imagery prior to getting out of bed each morning. Setting the alarm clock 5-10 minutes early will allow enough time to use imagery to plan and execute your daily goals. This will set the tone for a goal-focused day, as soon as your feet touch the floor at the start of each day!

3 Daily Goal Examples:

1) Practice imagery 10 minutes per day, 7 days a week.
2) Pack your lunch before going to bed.
3) Walk your dog.

Understanding the Goal Creation Process Using Your M.A.P.S Acronym

Measurable

Your motivational spirit is greatly strengthened, when progress can actually be seen. For example, an *achievement log* is a great vehicle for assisting you in creating your goals! This will also assist you with accountability and goal ownership.

Attainable

Avoid impossible goals; all goals should relate to where you are now, and you should aim to improve yourself one step at a time. If your goals prove unrealistic, then revaluate them. It is very important to define what is realistic because unrealistic goals lower motivation, decrease confidence, and do not provide you with a sense of accomplishment. It is not uncommon for someone to attempt to make up missing weeks or even years of exercise by engaging in unrealistic exercise programs that lead to injury. Remember, the goals you set should be controllable and challenging and also within the realm of possibility.

Personal

The goals you establish need to relate to you as an individual. Be clear in deciding what you want to achieve. Fully think through your goals so that you address various aspects of your performance that will contribute toward your long-term goal attainment.

Specific

Avoid setting unclear goals such as saying, "I want to lose some weight…" Be specific about how you want to improve and how you can measure it. For example, "I plan to lose 10 pounds in eight weeks by exercising 45 minutes a day, 4 days per week."

The Basic Framework for Implementing an Effective Goal-Setting Program:

Goal-Planning Phase

You set the stage for your efforts and actions. In this phase, you identify the direction your goals will take, in particular the specific means by which you will achieve your goals. Goal planning involves creating a mission statement in addition to the use of mental imagery to see and experience yourself achieving your ultimate goals.

Goal-Execution Phase

Self-instruction involves describing for yourself, either aloud or in writing, the specific steps to be performed to execute a given task, then completing the task at hand. Importantly noted here, daily goals are derived from your weekly goal plan.

Goal-Evaluation Phase

During this phase, you need to evaluate your development, determine what has worked, what has not worked, and identify needed adjustments to more effectively pursue and obtain your specified goals.

Creating a Compelling Vision!

Articulate and create a compelling vision of your desired future self; it is the foundation for planning. It provides the energy that moves you forward. It is the key that unlocks the door to your confidence when it comes to health, fitness, and overall well-being. By connecting with your best experiences and core values, it becomes much easier for you to visualize your way forward to a target that summons you. A compelling vision recognizes what you want rather than what you don't want.

Ask yourself the following 7 questions:

1) Why does this matter a lot to me, particularly right now?
2) What activities do I want to engage in consistently?
3) What abilities, talents, and strengths will I draw upon?
4) What challenges will I have the ability to overcome?
5) What results do I want to accomplish?
6) What support team and related structures will I establish?
7) Who do I want to be?

Key Point: Write your vision in the present tense, as if you have already realized it.

Effective Behavioral Goals

These goals are specific, measurable, action-oriented, realistic, and timed.

Important Points to Remember

"Trial and correction, not trial and error," represents a positive mindset for successfully accomplishing your goals!

Goals with a 3-month timeframe are medium-term goals, during which time you begin to learn and hopefully maintain a new set of behaviors. A 3-month timeframe is short enough to establish a sense of urgency for weekly goal setting, allowing you to mobilize your motivational spirit around meaningful and realistic actions and outcomes.

When clearly defining your goals, make sure to ask yourself what you want to be doing consistently in 3 months.

3 Goal-Achievement Strategies

1) Self-observation:
This is the monitoring of specific characteristics of your performance and/or daily habits, the surrounding conditions, and subsequent results.

2) Maintaining records:
Such examples of this strategy include the use of daily logs and sport journals, which are very efficient ways to identify whether or not you are effectively executing goal-related behavior.

3) Self-evaluation:
This is a very effective means of reflecting upon the adequacy of your degree of learning and performance.

Importantly Noted

Setting goals without brainstorming can decrease opportunities for fueling your motivation. Always record your goals once they have been identified.

Assessing Goal Importance

To assess if you are ready, willing, and able to make positive changes, it is vital to determine how important a goal is to you. Rate the importance of your goal on a scale of 0 to 10. Explore why you did not pick a lower number, also what it would take to create a higher number.

Self-Regulation

The more effective you become at self-regulating your priorities, behaviors, schedules, and time, the more likely you will be to adhere to your planned goals. Self-regulation strategies will provide you with control over your life. Once you perceive control over your behavioral outcomes, you are more able to successfully deal with challenges and barriers as they arise.

Self-Observation Systems

Such systems typically entail written or computer forms in which you record the behaviors you are seeking to change. Once you get accustomed to recordkeeping, it is also productive to take note of your thoughts and feelings, both helpful and unhelpful, that precede exercise and eating behaviors, for example.

Self-observation systems are beneficial to you in several ways. *First,* they increase your self-awareness. For example, you may not realize how many calories you consume while nibbling when you cook dinner or snacking when you watch television. Self-observation acts as a mirror so that you can get a much more objective view of your behavior. *Secondly,* self-monitoring will serve as a vital tool for evaluating your lifestyle behavior-change challenges and successes. *Third,* self-observation systems serve as a form of positive reinforcement and increase confidence.

Antecedents

An essential aspect of positive behavior change is realizing which behaviors have consequences under certain conditions. Antecedents are stimuli that come *before* a behavior and quite often signal the likely consequences of the behavior.

Antecedents assist in guiding your behaviors so that they will most likely lead to desirable or positive consequences. Also, antecedents can be manipulated to maximize the odds of desirable behaviors. This type of influence on behavior is called *stimulus control*; it can be a valuable tool for establishing positive behavior change. For example, if you frequently skip your workout sessions, a recommendation is to leave your gym bag in the front seat of your car; this is a visible reminder to go to the gym. As another example, you can keep healthy snacks in your desk at work, which will increase your chance of choosing something healthy versus buying unhealthy snacks at the vending machine. Having your gym bag and healthy snacks at your immediate access are examples of using stimulus control to modify behavior in a positive manner.

4 Stimulus-Control Strategy Examples

1) Keep a gym bag in your vehicle with all your necessary workout items.
2) Put a Post-It on your refrigerator door listing your daily goals/ reminders.
3) Be prepared by having clothes and shoes ready for early-morning workouts.
4) Carry or wear comfortable shoes to work so that you can take the stairs instead of the elevator, or you can take a walk during lunch.

7 Goal-Setting Obstacles

1) Creating too many goals too soon
2) Not taking into account individual differences, as there's not a one-size-fits-all approach to goal setting
3) Creating goals that are too general
4) Staying the course with unrealistic goals
5) Setting only outcome goals
6) Not fully understanding the time commitment
7) Not being able to create a supportive goal-setting environment can greatly impede goal (s) accomplishment.

Importantly noted, goal-setting obstacles can easily be avoided if you are able to recognize them at the beginning of the goal-setting process.

Why is the Concept of Control So Important to Setting Goals?

The concept of control to goal setting is of the utmost importance because setting realistic, attainable performance goals are within your control. When you possess *control* over your goal achievement, you are able to focus on your performance, often leading to subsequent outcome goal attainment, thus realizing your mission and vision and strengthening your motivational spirit!

Commitment

To realize your potential, somewhere deep in your core you must *choose* to go after your dreams. You also have to create and firmly establish an underlying belief that you can accomplish your goals. The plan is to nourish your focus, your confidence, long-term commitment, and belief in your mission statement. The fact is, dreams do not become a reality unless you act in ways that make them a reality.

Remember the Power of Accountability in Goal Setting

Accountability means taking the necessary steps to daily monitor and keep track of what was done, what happened, what worked, what did not work, and what you may want to do differently in the future. Accountability increases confidence, and confidence fuels motivation!

4 Personal Goals and Happiness Facts:[1]

1) Individuals who report a high degree of involvement and commitment to their goals exhibit a higher level of happiness and less stress.

2) Individuals who think that they can control the ways in which their goals proceed report higher levels of happiness than those who lack belief in personal control.
3) Choosing realistic and achievable goals is associated with happiness.
4) Individuals who have support from significant others (spouses, coworkers, classmates, or supervisors) report higher levels of happiness than those who receive less support.

Assertiveness

An effective strategy that can be utilized to assist you in achieving your goals is being more assertive; this is an important characteristic for achieving success and is defined as "the honest and straightforward expression of one's thoughts, feelings, and beliefs." [1] Usually, when people are not assertive, it is because they lack confidence. The more assertive you are regarding your concerns, struggles, progress, and accomplishments, the more likely you are to achieve long-term success and stay connected to your motivational spirit.

The 2 Ways in which We Approach and Perceive Goal Attainment

Task-Involved Individuals:

Task-involved people are concerned with the development of their competence in a self-reflective fashion. Ability is perceived as something that is improvable; therefore, satisfaction is obtained from performing at a level that extracts the very best of his or her ability by mastering a specific technique, increasing tactical awareness, or making personal improvements in a specified area.

Ego-Involved Individuals:

Ego-involved people perceive their ability as stable and fixed, thus limiting the effect that high levels of effort may have on their performance. Their goal is to show ability, often at the expense of effort. They judge themselves in comparison to others and have to establish superior ability in order to gain a positive view of themselves. In essence, to feel competent and successful, ego-involved individuals have to demonstrate ability superior to another person, regardless of personal improvements or developments that might have happened in the process of goal attainment.

Goal Attainment and Social Support:

Social support is the perceived emotional and physical comfort that an individual receives from others. There is evidence to support the motivational and adherence value in those who exercise regularly that have social support; it is possibly the most significant type of social influence on exercise adherence, for example. There are 4 types of social support consisting of: **1)** informational **2)** instrumental **3)** companionship and **4)** emotional.[2]

It is important for you to be aware of what type and amount of social support you currently require to adhere to and successfully achieve your established goals.

1) Informational Support

This type of support is one of the key reasons that people initially seek out personal trainers and health coaches, for example. This type of support includes advice, directions, or suggestions. How informational support is provided is also important. Informational support can also come from informal sources, such as family and friends who share their own similar experiences.

2) Instrumental Support

This is the practical and tangible aspects essential to help you adhere to exercise or achieve your goals. Some examples include transportation to a gym, a babysitter, or a spotter for weight training at the gym.

3) Companionship

This style of support is perhaps the most familiar type of support. Companionship support includes the availability of family, friends, and coworkers with whom you can pursue shared goals, such as exercising. Companionship during exercise yields positive feelings and might distract you from negative exercise-related feelings such as boredom, fatigue, pain, and distracting thoughts.

4) Emotional Support

This type of support is expressed through the use of encouragement, caring, concern, and empathy. Importantly noted, although emotional support goes a bit deeper, it can come in the form of an affirmation, which affirms intent and effort. Affirmations should be genuine and confirm something of value to you and be expressed in the present tense (as discussed in the Positive Thinking chapter).

Case Study Example: Kyle

Kyle is training to run his first marathon. He is 30 years old and in good physical condition. He ran track (100, 200, and 400 meters) during his high school and college years, thus he has a solid history in running, albeit a number of years ago. This marathon has been a lifelong goal of Kyle's, so he is very excited and enthusiastic to accomplish this goal.

Kyle was really pleased with his first month of training and believed that his goal of a 3-hour time for this marathon was appropriate. He is now toward the end of his second month of training and is feeling unsatisfied with his efforts. He has been doing his short runs for pace and is consistently running 8-minute miles. He is getting down on himself because he needs to be running 7-minute miles to finish the marathon in 3 hours. He is averaging 75 miles a week in training, and with all these miles accumulating, Kyle feels he should be getting stronger. However, he is actually averaging slower times.

He does not have a clear, well-defined training plan except to make sure he does long runs, intervals, and hill training. His mental goals of being positive and excited about training are practically nonexistent right now. In other words, his motivational spirit is essentially depleted. Kyle has a full-time job managing a car dealership and a relationship which he is also having difficulty balancing with his training schedule. He has five training weeks remaining and is interested in any information that I may have to help him achieve his goals. Kyle wants to fully connect to his motivational spirit because there is a very small chance that he will be able to run 26 miles, physically or mentally, the way he is feeling right now.

Assessing Kyle's Situation:

It seems that Kyle has not been utilizing a clear and structured program consisting of specifically defined goals. Due to this, it is quite possible that he is suffering from over-training, as 75 miles per week is most likely not recommended for a progressive training program leading up to a marathon. Also, Kyle is having difficulty managing his personal life with his training schedule, which is reflective of a motivational climate that prevents optimal training.

I would like to assist Kyle in setting performance goals because such goals are under his control; this is significant because the successful attainment of performance goals are necessary for the effective completion of outcome goals. A great way for Kyle to view performance goals is that they serve to build confidence and create a staircase to achieving long-term goals.

My primary goal is to help Kyle increase his self-awareness because, as discussed at the beginning of this chapter, gaining awareness is the first fundamental step to effective goal setting, not to give him a specific plan of action. If Kyle is not aware of the exact adjustments and training techniques that he needs to incorporate into his training, I will strongly suggest that he visit with a training coach to establish a clear, structured training program, in addition to learning more on his own time about specific areas to focus his marathon training efforts.

I suggest to Kyle that he break down his performance into a distinct number of controllable performances, using imagery. If he is able to successfully execute these behaviors, the likelihood of his reaching his long-term goal is greatly increased.

In the above example case study, as well as any goal directed behavior, it is vitally important to establish specific, attainable daily goals because *positive habits* are the end result!

Experiments have shown nearly all Habit Reminders fit into 1 or more of the following 5 categories:[3]

1) Immediately prior to the action (What action (s) proceeds the action/habit?)
2) Environment/location (Where are you?)
3) Emotional State (What is your emotional state?)
4) Time (What is the current time?)
5) Other People/Support (Who else is around?)

The fact is, habits do not actually disappear, even after a period of cessation; this is because habits are programmed into the neural pathways of our brain. If this were not the case, we would have to relearn how to play basketball after not having played for a short period of time, for example. What can be so problematic about this hardwiring of habits into the brain is that our brains can't distinguish between good and bad habits.

This explains why it can be very difficult to establish and maintain exercise habits or change our diet. For example, once we begin a routine, a habit of watching too much TV rather than going to the gym perhaps, or snacking too often, such patterns of behavior remain in our minds. However, if we learn to create positive *daily goals* that strengthen our motivational spirit, we then build new neurological routines that serve us well in our pursuits of accomplishing our long-term goals.

Closing Thought

By believing that you can change, creating a specific goal plan, and making it a habit, goals are accomplished, then positive changes become real; this is the amazing power of effective goal setting!

Chapter 4

Effective Communication and Team Cohesion:
Two Critical Aspects of Goal Attainment

"Have an understanding so there won't be a misunderstanding." —
Charles Blair

Effective Communication

This style of communication is a process, which entails sending, receiving, and interpreting messages through the 3 primary characteristics of effective communication; it is essential to the success of individuals and teams. It affects attitudes, expectations, emotional dispositions, behaviors, and motivation. The skill of being able to express your thoughts, feelings, and needs efficiently, and reciprocally to be able to understand the thoughts, feelings and ideas of others, is the *essence* of quality communication. When the communication process is working as it should, active listening leads to mutual understanding, trust, respect, and enhanced team cohesion.

The Three Primary Characteristics of Effective Communication[1]

1) 7% of effective communication is conveyed through *spoken words*.
2) 38% of effective communication is transmitted through your *tone of voice*.
3) 55% of effective communication is conveyed through *body language*.

Important Point to Ponder

More than 90% of our communication that we convey to others has nothing to do with what we say!

The essence of how we communicate can be characterized by both verbal and non-verbal communication. Understanding the significance and proper application of each can greatly influence your ability to deliver the message that you intend successfully when communicating.

Effective Communication Insights

When you make eye contact while communicating you are establishing an important aspect of nonverbal communication. Research has discovered that maintaining reasonable (compared to constant or no) eye contact with others usually creates positive feelings in the person with whom you are communicating. Research also indicates that individuals engage in more eye contact when they are listening compare to when they are speaking. There is also a cultural component to keep in mind when making eye contact; for example, direct eye contact can be perceived as an insult in Latin America and Japan.[2]

It is important to understand and be mindful of the fact that cultural and personal beliefs have the potential to greatly impact the meaning that others abstract from messages. For example, our brains organize incoming sensations into a mental map, which represents our uniquely individual perception of reality. If an incoming piece of information does not fit into our perception of what is being communicated, our brains may take the shortcut and simply distort the information in an effort to make it fit our currently held beliefs, a phenomenon known as *selective perception*.[3] Having this awareness allows us to take a step back, think, and expand our perspective on pre-held beliefs and notions. Additionally, presenting information in a concise, effective manner shows respect for other people's time and increases the odds of your message being well received, accompanied by a positive response.

Conveying Negative Information Effectively

Negative information should *not* be conveyed to others or teammates without any type of explanation or justification because team cohesion is predicated on respect and effective communication.

4 Listening Styles

1) Active Listening
This style of listening entails being tuned in to what the speaker has to say, connecting with the individual, engaged in the conversation, and showing a desire to genuinely understand what is being said.

2) Inattentive Listening
This type of listening occurs when the listener stops listening because they feel they understand what is being said. If listening in this fashion, a general idea might be grasped; however, large pieces most likely will be missed—for example, underlying concepts.

3) Arrogant Listening
An arrogant listening style highlights those who are more interested in what they have to say instead of what the other individual involved in the conversation is saying.

4) Reflective Listening
This form of listening is one of the most powerful ways of showing someone that you are actively listening and are genuinely interested in what they have to say.

The Reflective Listening Process

1) Questioning
Utilize open-ended questions. For example, "Will you please tell me a little more about what happened?"

2) Clarifying
Make clear to the person speaking what you heard them say. For example, "What I hear you say is…it sounds like…"

3) Encouraging
Make use of both verbal and nonverbal communication to facilitate the speaker to continue to expand on their thoughts. For example, nodding your head in agreement or repeating a key word.

4) Paraphrasing
Rephrase the speaker's main points to check whether you understand their message by using concise comments back to the speaker, referencing the essence of their message.

5) Reflecting
Simply letting the speaker know that you can hear the feelings and the content of what is being said. For example, "You are angry about not making the final cut, and feel you were not given a fair assessment by Coach Watkins."

6) Understanding
This entails using empathy to keep the speaker focused on key issues. For example, "It must be very difficult for you to sit on the bench and watch your teammates practice while you are recovering from an ACL injury. I experienced the same season-ending injury during my freshman year of college. I can relate to what you are going through."

7) Summarizing
This involves putting together all the main ideas and feeling of what the speaker said. For example, "You are pleased with your injury rehabilitation process, learned a great deal about your resiliency and motivation, plan to continue your daily goals, and make necessary adjustments, as needed. You also wish to help others who encounter similar setbacks in the future."

Effective Communication Tip:

Begin a conversation in a friendly way. "In talking with people, don't begin by discussing the things on which you differ. Begin by emphasizing and keep emphasizing the things on which you agree. Keep emphasizing, if possible, that you are both striving for the same end and that your only difference is one of method and not of purpose."[4]

Major Factors Affecting Effective Communication:

Both *personal* and *situational* factors impact the process of communication. Your personality, beliefs, upbringing, values, personal mannerisms, and style of communicating interact with a variety of situation specific circumstances to influence the way messages are conveyed and received. *Contextual* factors entail your relationship with the other person.

Other factors, including *stress* and *selective attention*, can impact the way information is expressed, received, and interpreted. Often when interpreting verbal and non-verbal messages, information might be lost or distorted. As well, we often think we hear a person say one thing when, in fact, they said something completely different. Subsequently, acting based on what we think the person said can and does cause many communication problems and misunderstandings.

Team Cohesion

This is a dynamic process that is reflected in the propensity for a group to stick together and remain united in efforts to obtain a collective goal. Cohesiveness can be built or enhanced, and it can fluctuate. Communication between team members and group leaders, such as coaches, often become strained, affecting goal commitment and team cohesion.

4 Factors that affect Team Cohesion

1) Personal factors
Such factors have to do with the characteristics of the individuals who make up the team or group. Quite possibly the most significant

personal factor connected with the development of both task and team cohesion in sports is *individual satisfaction*. The quality of the competition is one aspect; having opportunities for social interactions with your teammates is another. In efforts to feel satisfied, athletes need to feel that they are improving in skill. Satisfaction is derived from the recognition of others: coaches, parents, teammates, and fellow students. The coach's relationship with the athlete is a potential source of satisfaction or dissatisfaction. The extent to which athletes engage in practice is another important personal factor connected to team cohesion. When these elements are optimally satisfied, team cohesion is greatly enhanced.

2) Team factors

Team factors represent the aspects of the group that have to do with having a stronger bond, due to being in the group. Within every team, there are two categories of roles, *formal* (roles that are clearly defined by the team, such as coach, team captain, or manager, as well as certain positions within the team) and *informal* (formed from the interactions that the team/group has, such as the team clown, etc.) Informal roles can be positive or negative.

It is essential for you to understand 4 aspects of your role as a team member: **1**) what your role entails, **2**) behaviors that are required to fulfill your role responsibilities, **3**) how your role performance will be evaluated, and **4**) what consequences should ensue if responsibilities are not fulfilled. Importantly noted, role involvement is associated with group cohesiveness to the extent to which athletes, individuals, or workers *accept* their role responsibilities.

3) Leadership factors

These factors involve behaviors of the team leader and relationships that team members have with the leader, in addition to the leader's style. The interrelationship among the athlete, the coach, the amount of cohesiveness, and performance are multifaceted. The coaches' decision style can also have an impact on the amount of cohesiveness within a team.

4) Situational factors

Situational factors include the setting the sport takes place in, the social setting, and structural aspects of the team/group. A situational factor connected to the development of team cohesion is *distinctiveness*. Traditionally, distinctiveness is established through such means as team mottos and uniforms. As a set of individuals become more distinctive from others, feelings of unity increase, thereby facilitating team cohesion.

5 Activities for Building Effective Communication and Cohesion within Your Team or Group

1) Role-play

This is a great activity to do with groups because it gets every team member engaged in the activity, mutually working together, building team cohesion. With role-play, you get a chance to practice how you would like things to go. You can do role-plays with made-up scenarios to practice various skills (such as reflective listening) or real-life game situations to help gain confidence at communicating effectively. Role-plays can be performed either one in front of the whole group or many happening at once. Importantly noted, remember to discuss what happened. When discussing, get feedback from all parties about how communication went.

2) Discussion

Very often, the most successful work around communication occurs in a discussion format. By discussing as a group what is working and what is not, insights into team dynamics and the current level of cohesion are revealed. Group discussions are an excellent time to practice active listening skills, as well.

3) Icebreakers
These activities do what the name suggests: "break the ice." These are typically quick, nonthreatening, get-to-know-one-another activities; for example, name games, or games where you learn similarities or differences about the other people on your team. You could simply share 3 things about yourself that you are proud of or enjoy that none of your teammates, classmates, or coworkers know about.

4) Back-to-back game
Communication is at the foundation of this game. In this activity, you and another team member sit back to back. Person A draws a picture that person B cannot see, for example a picture of a baseball stadium, full of fans. Then person A has to explain to person B how to draw the picture.

5) Team contract
The goal is to brainstorm what rules you want to establish as a team. Team contracts are beneficial when you are on the field, at team meetings, and in other aspects of your sport. It is key that after brainstorming, *before* team commitment to the contract, that *all members* of the team feel comfortable with what is on the contract. Once you have finalized the contract as a team, have *every* team member sign it, and then provide copies to the team/group; this process increases commitment on behalf of the individual players to the team's shared goals.

Remember:
Fostering team cohesion means collectively working together in efforts to direct your focus toward accomplishing your shared goals and dreams as a team; this will increase your team's odds of success.

Recognizing Illogical Arguments
Another aspect of refining your communication skills is being able to quickly recognize an illogical argument because effective

communication is based upon having a clear understanding of the speaker's message. Formalizing your reasoning has the propensity to lead to useful benefits, such as greater clarity of thought, as well as improved objectivity. Additionally, if you possess the skill to analyze others' arguments, you can use this as a means of knowing when to just simply withdraw from a conversation or a discussion that will probably be unsuccessful—in essence, a waste of your time.

The following are 6 of the more notable logical fallacies that present an irrelevant topic in efforts to divert attention away from the specific issue at hand.

1) Straw man

To create a straw man is to deliberately caricature individuals' argument with the goal of attacking the caricature as opposed to the actual argument. Misquoting, misrepresenting, and oversimplifying someone's message are ways in which this fallacy is committed. The straw man argument is typically more ridiculous than the actual argument, thus making it easier to attack. It also serves the diversionary tactic of luring the other person to defend the more outlandish, hence illogical, argument rather than their original point.

Example: "Senator Hill thinks we should modify the penal system. I cannot believe he wants to let murderers out of prison!"

2) Ad hominem

This illogical argument attacks the person instead of the message he or she is attempting to make; the goal is to divert the discussion and totally discredit their message.

Example: "Who cares what Dr. Jones says about your medication? Dr. Jones is a liar who has cheated on both of his previous wives!"

3) Appeal to ignorance

This type of argument assumes a suggestion to be true simply because there is no evidence proving that it is untrue.

Example: "You can't prove that Sasquatch doesn't exist; therefore, it must!"

4) Circular reasoning

This occurs when someone indirectly or clearly assumes the conclusion is either deliberately utilized as a premise, or more often, it is reworded to look as though it is a different suggestion when in fact it is not.

Example: Susan told her math teacher, "You can't give me a C; I am an A student!"

5) Slippery slope

This type of argument tries to discredit a suggestion by arguing that its acceptance will certainly lead to a sequence of events, one or more of which are unwanted and undesirable.

Example: "If marijuana is legalized, then everyone will start doing cocaine and heroin. Theft will increase; thus, the moral fabric of our country will be forever damaged…don't you see?!"

6) Appeal to irrelevant authority

This illogical argument attempts to appeal to a person's sense of modesty; it is basically an appeal to the feeling that others are more educated and well-informed.

Example: "Oprah Winfrey says it's unhealthy to eat after 8:00 p.m.; therefore, it must be true!"

Emotions High-Logic Low

One of the key takeaways from this book is the reminder that our thoughts impact our feelings. Subsequently, our feelings affect our behavior, hence our habits and goals. There is a strong effect for emotionally charged topics and deeply rooted beliefs, which results in individuals tending to interpret ambiguous suggestions as supporting their position. This can lead to *confirmation bias*, which is the tendency to favor information that confirms one's beliefs while dismissing any and all information that does not confirm those beliefs.

It is worth emphasizing again, formalizing your logical reasoning has the propensity to lead to useful benefits, such as improved clarity of thought, which increases your ability to optimally focus on your goals!

Closing Thought

Any message that you attempt to convey contains a piece of you!

Chapter 5

Stress and Anxiety:
Barriers to Achieving Your Goals

You might think stress is something that happens to you, like when you try to juggle five tasks at once, or your boss tells you that tomorrow's work was due yesterday, or you lose a loved one. The reality is stress doesn't come from the outside world; we create stress through our perception of situations and events.

Defining Stress and Understanding the Process

According to McGrath[1] stress is defined as "a substantial imbalance between demand (physical and/or psychological) and response capability, under conditions where failure to meet that demand has important consequences." Stress is essentially a process consisting of a sequence of events, which lead to a specific end. McGrath proposed a relatively simple model of stress, consisting of 4 interrelated steps: environmental demand, perception of demand, stress response, and behavioral consequences.[2]

Step 1: Environmental Demand

The first step of the stress process involves some type of demand being placed on a person. The demand may be psychological or physical—for example, a high school volleyball player has to execute a newly learned skill in front of the team, or perhaps when parents and friends are pressuring you to win a 5K race.

Step 2: Perception of Demand

The second step of the stress response is a person's perception of the psychological or physical demand. As human beings, we do not perceive demands in exactly the same manner. For example, two ninth graders might view having to give a five-minute presentation in front of their class quite differently. Mary might enjoy the attention of being in front of the class, whereas Susan may feel nervous. That is, Susan perceives an imbalance between the demands put on her (having to present in front of the class) and her ability to actually meet those demands. Mary perceives no such imbalance or perceives it only to a minimal degree.

Step 3: Stress Response

The third step of the stress response is the person's psychological and physical response to their perception of a given situation. If an individual's perception of an imbalance between demands and response ability causes them to feel threatened, increased anxiety results, thus bringing with it increased uncertainties, and heightened physiological activation. Individuals have a decreased ability to concentrate and increased level of muscle tension, when experiencing an increase in anxiety levels.

Step 4: Behavioral Consequences

The fourth step is the actual behavior of the person under distress. For example, a high school soccer player perceives an imbalance between ability and demands and feels an increased level of anxiety. Does their performance deteriorate? Or does the increased level of anxiety that they are experiencing increase intensity of effort, thus improving performance? Good question…

The fact is, the final step of the stress process cycles back into the first. Let's say a student becomes overly worried and performs poorly in front of their class. The other children might laugh; this negative social assessment then becomes an additional demand on the student (step 1). The stress process then develops into a continuing cycle of negativity.[2]

The Relationship between our Thoughts and Stress

The fact is high levels of stress impacts our memory and attention. Let's take a closer look as to how this happens.

Stress has the potential to impair cognitive functioning to varying degrees, quite often by distracting our attention. An often overlooked fact that many of us tend to not give the attention that it needs is that noise can be a stressor; this can be chronic for individuals who live in noisy environments, such as next to a freeway or train tracks. How does chronic noise impact cognitive performance? Many individuals attempt to deal with the stressful effects of noise by changing the focus of their attention from the source of the noise to relevant aspects of the task at hand, they essentially "tune out" the noise, as much as they possibly can. Research by Cohen et al. (1986)[3] suggests that children who make attempts to tune out chronic noise are susceptible to developing generalized cognitive deficits because they have trouble knowing which sounds to apply their attention to and which ones to tune out.[4]

An interesting piece of research discovered that individuals who were living in close proximately to the Three Mile Island nuclear power plant in Pennsylvania when a major nuclear accident happened still experienced stress from the accident many years later; however, others did not. Why is this? The answer is, those individuals who continued to feel distressed had difficulty keeping thoughts about the accident and their associated fears out of their minds; it seems quite likely that these thoughts caused their stress and, in many instances, made it chronic.[4] This is an excellent example of how our thoughts affect our feelings, and our feelings impact our behavior.

Point to Ponder:

"Most of our tensions and frustrations stem from compulsive needs to act the role of someone we are not...Resolve to be thyself; and know that he who finds himself, loses his misery."

—Hans Selye, prominent pioneer in stress research [5]

Defining Anxiety

Anxiety often feels like a sense of disquiet, as if constant vigilance is the only hope of avoiding this negative state. There are numerous forms of anxiety. Generalized anxiety disorder is self-explanatory; it's generalized, compared to phobias which focus on specific things and situations. In individuals with panic attacks, the anxiety becomes overwhelming, boiling over with a paralyzing, hyperventilating sense of impending crisis, which facilitates an enormous activation of the sympathetic nervous system. In obsessive-compulsive disorder, individuals exhibit endless patterns of distracting rituals, searching for a sense of calm. Characteristically, in post-traumatic stress disorder, the source of anxiety can be linked to a specific trauma. Importantly noted, none of these types of anxiety is about fear because the foundation of the phenomenon of fear is the vigilance as well as the need to escape from something real. The essence of anxiety is about dread and worry, the imagination running wild and uncontrollably from one negative thought to the next. As with depression, anxiety is based upon cognitive distortions.[6]

The unfortunate reality is, anxiety is part of our lives to varying degrees; it seems there's always something to fret and worry about, stress often awaiting to compound the impact of anxiety. Fortunately, we aren't all anxious, worrying about everything. Some people are "cool as a cucumber," seeming to simply take things in stride. It is no surprise that an individual's typical level of anxiety is a fairly stable personality characteristic, which is an important element of one's temperament.

We all have our own unique individual anxiety level, unique in that we each experience and respond to our environment, often quite differently than others. A core characteristic of anxiety is that it is very subjective. What is very stressful to one individual might hardly matter to someone else. If only it were as simple as just having the ability to not stress over the "small stuff" in life, or things outside our control...

The fact is, individuals who are predisposed to experience excessive amounts of anxiety perceive much of what they encounter in their daily lives as stressful, compared to less anxious people who choose to not focus on the "small stuff." Such differences happen because of the sole combination of genes we acquire from our two parents, in addition to the unique experiences that we have as we travel the path of life. It is true that anxiety and fear are perfectly normal experiences of life; however, they have the potential to become maladaptive, thus increasing in frequency and or duration. When this occurs, the result is a significant increase in distress to the extent that daily life is negatively impacted.[7]

Remember:

"Anxiety's like a rocking chair. It gives you something to do, but it doesn't get you very far."

—Jodi Picoult[7]

Identifying Sources of Stress

Stress comes at us from many directions with thousands of sources. Research has highlighted that major life events, such as a career change or death of a loved one, as well as daily hassles of life, such as your vehicle breaking down or an issue with a coworker, cause stress and impact both mental and physical health.[2]

In athletes, potential stressors include performance issues, negative thinking, excessively worrying about performing up to abilities and expectations, self-doubts about level of talent; situational issues, such as financial costs or the amount of time required for training; organizational issues, such as a lack of effective communication and coaching leadership; and relationships or stressful experiences outside of sport, for example, negative interpersonal relationships.

Research has also found that injured elite athletes are susceptible to experiencing psychological stressors that involve a loss of hope and self-identity. Although there are thousands of specific stressors, for those participating in competitive sport or simply navigating everyday life, these stressors are determined by both personality and the particular situation at hand.[2]

Situational Stress

Situational stress consists of 2 general areas. The first is the significance placed on a competition or event, and the second is the uncertainty that surrounds the possible outcome of that event.[2]

1) Event Significance

Typically, the more important the event, the greater the likelihood that the event will present some degree of stress. Following this premise, a championship competition is considerably more stressful than a regular-season game, just as taking a college exam is more stressful than taking a practice test.

The significance placed on a competition or event is not always obvious. An event that might seem insignificant to a majority of people might be very significant for one particular person. For example, a regular-season basketball game might not seem particularly important to most players on a team that has secured a spot in the championship game. Yet it might be of major importance to Paul, a player who is being observed by several college scouts. When evaluating the source of stressors, it is beneficial to continually assess the significance that you attach to activities, various tasks, events, and/or competitions.

2) Uncertainty

Uncertainty is a significant situational source of stress, and the greater the degree of uncertainty, the greater the stress experienced. Quite often, we cannot do anything to prevent the uncertainty that occupies many situations. For instance, when two evenly matched teams are scheduled to compete, there is a very high degree of uncertainty. However, little can or should be done about it. After all, the essence of competition is about having evenly matched opponents. Unfortunately, there are times when teachers and coaches create unnecessary uncertainty by not informing their student athletes of such things as the starting lineups, how to avoid injury in learning high-risk physical skills, or what to expect while rehabilitating from a serious sport-related injury. Coaches and teachers would benefit from being aware of how they might unknowingly create uncertainty in their athletes.

The fact is uncertainty is not limited to sport participation or the gym. Athletes and exercisers sometimes feel the effects of stress as a result of uncertainty in their lives outside of their exercise lives. For instance, a study of Australian football players discovered that uncertainty about one's future after their football career ended, such as possible relocation, as well as work and nonwork struggles were significant sources of stress.[2] Be vigilant and watch for uncertainty because it creates a feeling of threat to our confidence and motivational spirit.

The Destructive Nature of Stress and Anxiety

While we experience stress our body's ability to grow and repair tissue is impaired, and sexual drive is decreased for both men and women. In addition to these changes, our immunity is also negatively impacted, resulting in a weakened immune system. With adequate activation, the stress response itself can become considerably more damaging than the stressor itself in many instances, particularly when the stress is purely psychological. This is a very important concept because it is correlated with the rise of stress-related disease.[6] The reality is, if you live your daily life in a heightened state of stress, your odds of getting sick are increased.

The Effects of Temporarily Severe Stress on Proper Brain Functioning

Bruce McEwen, known for his impressive work in the field of the biology of stress, has demonstrated through his research that severe but temporary stress can potentially result in a shortening of dendrites in the hippocampus. Dendrites serve very important functions, as they are part of the neurons that receive incoming signals, as well as being responsible for memory formation. McEwen has also demonstrated through his research that if stressors are removed, these changes are reversible.[8]

The Effects of Chronic Stress on the Brain

You may wonder, "How does sustained stress impact proper functioning of our brain?" According to Robert M. Sapolsky in his book *Behave: The Biology of Humans at Our Best and Worst,* "Stress causes dendritic reaction and synapse loss, lower levels of NCAM (a 'neural cell adhesion molecule' that stabilizes synapses). The more of these changes, the more attentional and decision-making impairments occur" [9]

Unfortunately, with chronic stress, the hippocampus region of the brain starts to weaken and falter in its capacity to control the release of stress hormones, and to complete its routine functions. Permanent changes occur; cells in the hippocampus start to degenerate, and the result is permanent memory loss. The destructive impact of stress on the hippocampus was initially discovered by Robert Sapolsky; he had conducted research on the effects of *social stress* on the behavior of monkeys. "The monkeys lived in a colony as social subordinates to a dominate male. Over several years, some died. Upon autopsy, they were found to have stomach ulcers, consistent with their having lived under stress-provoking conditions. Most dramatically, though, it was discovered that marked degeneration of the hippocampus had occurred. There was little sign of damage to any other part of the brain. This basic finding has been confirmed in a number of situations."[8]

Additional studies using rats revealed that, under stressful conditions, they were unable to learn and remember how to do behavioral tasks, which depend on the hippocampus. For instance, the stressed rats were unable to learn the specific location of the safe platform utilized in the study. Prolonged, sustained stress interferes with our ability to induce long-term potentiation in the hippocampus region of our brains, which most likely explains why memory fails under such conditions.[8]

Recognizing the Importance of Control

When attempting to minimize and control the negative effects of stress on our lives, we need to recognize and be fully aware of the importance of control. Controlling the benefits and rewards that you receive from your daily pursuits, or lack thereof, can be more desirable than getting what you seek for nothing. For instance, an interesting piece of research revealed that pigeons as well as rats preferred to press a lever to get food over having the food simply delivered to them; this type of behavior is also seen in human beings because there is a greater *purpose* and *meaning* in the striving and the continual pursuit of goal attainment.[6] The cornerstone of this phenomenon is deriving a sense of accomplishment and purpose from possessing *control* over our thoughts and actions, and the meaningful reward that accompanies the pursuit of our goals.

The Impact of Strong Negative Emotions

A strong, negative emotion such as anger doubles your risk of a heart attack during the following two hours.[6] When we experience a lack of control in our lives, less predictive information is available to us to make the best decision; there is a close relationship between a loss of control and predictive information. The fact is, predictive information allows us to gain more control, and to recognize what internal coping approach is most likely to work best during a stressful situation.

Our response to stress results in a variety of biological and psychological changes with the goal of preparing the body for "fight-or-flight" situations. Once the stress response occurs, a waterfall of biochemical changes happen in the adrenal, hypothalamus, and pituitary glands, in addition to the sympathetic nervous system. These biochemicals facilitate the psychological and physical changes we experience during the stress response.[10]

The Essence of Stress Management

The essence of stress management is defined as the thoughts and methods we use to deal with stress. There are 2 general methods of managing stress: emotion-focused and problem-focused.

1) Emotion-focused

The focus here is concerned with reducing the level of emotional distress experienced, particularly when changing the situation is not an option. Emotion-focused stress management strategies involve efforts to minimize the problem/issues or find a positive aspect to the situation by such practices as exercising or talking with friends.

2) Problem-focused

The goal of this stress management strategy is to define the demand, create solutions, and take specific actions needed to reduce, eliminate, or turn the perceived problem into a nonissue. For example, Mike, a high school student dealing with the stress of the possibility of receiving a D in his math class, might respond by seeking assistance from his math teacher, adopting consistent study habits, and joining a study group; these are all excellent examples of problem-focused stress management strategies for Mike to utilize.

The Stress Response in Practice

Let's say, for example, Tony, a corporate fitness expert, is asked by his company's personnel director to help create a stress management program for the company's employees. **Step 1** recommends that he should determine what *demands* are placed on the employees (e.g., increased workloads, hectic travel schedules, and or unrealistic scheduling demands). An examination of **Step 2** may lead Tony to question *who* is experiencing or perceiving the most stress (e.g., people in specific departments or with certain jobs, or those individuals with certain personality temperaments). **Step 3** is about studying the *reactions* the employees are having to the increased anxiety and concentration issues resulting in chronic stress. **Step 4** analysis focuses on the ensuing *behavior* of employees feeling increased stress—for example, decreased job satisfaction, absenteeism, and, or reduced job productivity.

With the information gathered from the 4 steps, Tony can specifically target his efforts to reduce employee stress. He may recommend physical activity (most likely in step 3) or other means of stress reduction—for example, restructuring of work schedules. Understanding the 4-step stress response, Tony has a significantly better grasp of the specific causes and negative consequences of stress, thus allowing him to create and design a more effective stress-reduction goal plan for the company's employees.

3 Excellent Stress Management Tools

1) Exercise
This stress reduction tool assists in countering stress and decreases your risk of numerous cardiovascular and metabolic diseases. Also, exercise typically makes people feel good; it has a revitalizing effect on mind and body, especially when made into a daily habit. Alternatively, too much exercise can lead to additional stressors, such as injury, fatigue, and a lack of enjoyment; therefore, you should have an attainable exercise plan that is fun and personalized.

2) Control
The more certainty, predictive information about current and possible future stressors you possess, will allow you the opportunity to devise and establish both emotion- and problem-focused stress reduction strategies, thereby gaining control of how you respond to stress. *Possessing control and working to create certainty in your goal pursuits is a foundational theme of this book.

3) Effort
The act itself of putting forth an effort mentally (gaining awareness) and behaviorally (acting on this awareness) reduces stress levels; hence, motivation decreases stress.

How Might Social Support Impact Our Health?
In regard to workplace stress, research conducted by Karlin, Brondolo & Schwartz (2003)[11] discovered that social support had a considerably stronger association with lower blood pressure during stressful times.

According to Wills & Fegan (2001)[12] the impact of social support on our health can by answered by two theories: "direct effects" and the "buffering" hypothesis. The buffering hypothesis asserts that social support influences our health by protecting us against the negative impact of high levels of stress.

Buffering works in two ways. *First*, when individuals encounter a strong stressor such as a financial crisis, those who possess a high degree of social support might be less likely to evaluate the situation as stressful, compared to those with a low degree of social support. People with a high degree of social support might expect or know for a fact that someone they know will assist them, either by giving them sound advice on how to get money or lending it to them. *Second*, social support might modify an individual's response to a stressful occurrence after the initial assessment. For example, people with a reasonable degree of social support may have someone greatly assist them in finding answers and solutions to their problem, quite possibly convincing them that the stressor is not very significant. At the very least, having someone providing social support contributes toward a "look on the bright side," kind of thinking, often resulting in positive thinking and reduced stress levels. Comparatively, individuals with low levels of social support are far less likely to have any such advantages, thus experiencing a greater impact from their stressors.[4]

The direct effects theory purposed by Wills & Fegan (2001)[12] asserts that social support benefits our health and happiness regardless of the amount of stress we experience. You may be wondering, just how does direct effects work? One way is that individuals with high levels of social support tend to have strong feelings of confidence and belongingness; the positive outlook this produces is known to be beneficial to our health independent of stress levels. Studies have found lower blood pressure levels in both daily life and laboratory tests among middle-aged individuals with higher levels of social support regardless of the amount of stress experienced. Other evidence suggests that high levels of support tend to encourage people to lead healthy lifestyles (Broman,

1993; Peirce et al., 2000).[13] When we have a strong support system in place, we are far more inclined to exercise and lead healthy lives because others care about us and need us in their lives.[12]

Social support also enables the production of protein-based molecules, such as T-cells and natural killer cells, which assist with proper immune functioning. Social support seems to slow many processes associated with body and brain aging. In a study of approximately 7,000 subjects, it was discovered that individuals with more social support live longer regardless of their socioeconomic status, exercise habits, smoking, or obesity. The results of this study support the fact that social support improves our health by assisting in regulating our emotions, which subsequently has a positive impact on metabolism and immunological functioning.[14]

The Importance of Social Support during the Rehabilitation Process

The role of social support during the rehabilitation process acts as a specific means to recover lost or diminished resources. A wide range of socially supportive behaviors, including positive goal-oriented encouragement, reassurance, and personal assistance maintaining passion for the sport and other goals, all serve to keep the injured individual connected to their motivational spirit while they navigate their way through the rehabilitation process.

Social support that encourages athletes to participate in team activities greatly helps maintain a sense of involvement. Fluctuating motivation is normal throughout the injury rehabilitation process; social support can help with such ebb-and-flow moments by providing encouragement and positive feedback. [15] Social support is vital in helping athletes cope with injury-related demands in maintaining motivation to adhere to rehabilitation protocols, and in facilitating emotional adjustment to these new demands. The benefits of social support can also be seen in the form of role models, including those who have the ability to provide emotional comfort, inspiration, and motivation to manage and overcome injury rehabilitation obstacles and setbacks.[16]

Specifically, 4 types of social support can assist in navigating through the injury rehabilitation process: **1**) **emotional** (showing empathy), **2**) **informational** (providing the necessary information), **3**) **tangible** (driving you to and from rehabilitation), and **4**) **motivational** (genuine encouragement).

Remember:

Social support increases an individual's chance of successful implementation and continued utilization of emotion- and problem-based coping skills. It is vital to understand that a solid support system consisting of people serving different roles throughout the rehabilitation process is an essential element to a successful rehabilitation program.

Case Study Example: Cheryl

Cheryl is a soccer player and has been playing soccer since she was 9 years old. In high school, she was very competitive and was recruited by numerous colleges to play soccer for their teams. Although it wasn't her 1st choice, Cheryl ultimately chose the college that offered her the best scholarship. Cheryl is now a senior and has been starting for the soccer team since her sophomore year. At the end of the season last year during a game, she landed awkwardly on her left leg. She felt her knee pop and then felt intense pain and immediately knew she had suffered a significant injury to her knee. After receiving an MRI, the doctors discovered that she had torn her ACL and would require surgery.

Cheryl is a senior and knows that this will most likely be her last year of playing competitive soccer. When she had her preseason individual meeting with her coach, she was not cleared for practice and could only do drills that didn't require quick stops and starts or rapidly changing directions. During the meeting, upon hearing that

Cheryl wasn't cleared yet to return to full game play, coach Fisher began to talk to her about what the team strategy would be if she was going to be unable to play and who would be filling her spot on the team. Cheryl was distressed by this comment and hurt that coach Fisher didn't acknowledge just how much work she had done so far to rehabilitate from her injury.

Cheryl is now back practicing with the soccer team. She has been fully cleared by her doctor to return to competitive play. Sally, her trainer suggested that she play with a hinged knee brace. Cheryl hates playing with the brace because she says it feels awkward and uncomfortable, but she's also nervous about reinjuring her knee. Even though the brace feels awkward, she feels comfortable with fast, swift movements. Cheryl also has concerns of someone sliding towards her during game play, making her panic at various times. She also thinks that Coach Fisher is not confident in her and is worried that during her last year as a college soccer player, she'll be watching the games from the sidelines instead of actually playing.

Assessing Cheryl's Issues

Cheryl is having difficulty adjusting to her injury. For example, she hates playing with the brace because she says it feels awkward, *but* she's also nervous about reinjuring her knee. The fact that Cheryl is having such difficulties adjusting to her injury after almost a year "raises a red flag," as it pertains to her stress management skills.

In assessing what *personal factors* that may be present for Cheryl, the following concerns should be addressed. Several personal factors often interact, as in Cheryl's situation. She has been playing soccer on a consistent basis since she was nine years old as a very competitive athlete. This brings into question her *athletic identity*; athletes who derive their self-worth from sport participation are at greater-risk for lacking the necessary coping skills, in addition to becoming more susceptible to the possible clinical issues that can arise post-injury. She is experiencing symptoms of denial and distress, representative of inadequate coping skills. It does not appear that she has prior experience with such injuries. Combining the mentioned personal factors with her early specialization in sport creates a "recipe" for possibly the most significant factor, Cheryl's *level of confidence*. She possesses limited coping skills, possibly an over-identification of self-worth tied to her chosen sport; this greatly impacts Cheryl's confidence.

In terms of the various *situational significant factors* that are of concern for Cheryl are the timing, severity, and length of the injury. Cheryl is now a senior; the timing of this injury is influencing her participation, as she knows that this will probably be her last year of playing competitive soccer. She suffered a torn ACL; this is a severe injury, requiring a lengthy rehabilitation process, impacting her daily activities and related goals, thus creating life stress. The *life stress* variable is strengthened by this being her senior year as an athlete, as well as not feeling like she is receiving social support from Coach Fisher.

Establishing a Plan for Cheryl

The *first* step in creating a plan for Cheryl is establishing an understanding of the possible clinical issues than can arise from her injury, especially since there are numerous personal and situational factors involved in this case. A clear understanding will be conveyed as to how *understanding* these issues can have a significant influence on the length of recovery time, reentry into the sport, and ultimate success of the rehabilitation program.

The *second* step is essentially addressing her overall level of self-confidence. This is the core task because an athlete's level of confidence can affect their belief in their treatment program, their ability to stick to the program, as well as their ability to fully recover and successfully return to their sport. Such concerns as fear of not being able to perform as well and fear of being reinjured contribute to an athlete's lack of confidence. For example, Cheryl is nervous about reinjuring her knee. She is also exhibiting a minimal amount of control over the situation;

cognitive distortions are reflected in her portraying the reaction of Coach Fisher in a negative light. These factors contribute to Cheryl having a low level of confidence.

My primary focus here is to help Cheryl successfully navigate through her rehabilitation program, considering the ability to *adhere* to a rehabilitation program is the key factor influencing successful recovery from injury. I will assist her in gaining a sense of *control* over her situation, and assuming personal responsibility for the success of her injury rehabilitation program.

The specific strategies that will be utilized are *emotion-focused* and *problem-focused* coping because Cheryl is having problems coping, adjusting, and accepting her injury. Emotion-focused coping will *reduce* the intensity and frequency of Cheryl's psychological and behavioral responses, which will serve to promote 6 perceived positive outcomes.[17] These positive outcomes entail the utilization of 6 different perspectives. **1**) A *common-place perspective* involves being able to confide in others, such as Cheryl's family and friends. **2**) A *manageability perspective* considers how things could be worse; it is realistic that her injury could have been more severe. **3**) A *personal perspective* recalls long-term aspirations and hopes and recognizes how these events fit into them. Cheryl needs to consider her aspirations outside her athletic identity. **4**) Assuming a *time perspective* anticipates a time when events will be over. Such a perspective will allow Cheryl to see a realistic period for a return to a state of normalcy. **5**) A *global perspective* compares her situation as a whole to a global circumstance. **6**) A *positive perspective* involves seeking positive aspects of the experience. Cheryl can learn from her rehabilitation process, thus seeking preventive measures to avoid possible overuse injuries in the future, while strengthening her motivational spirit in the process.

Cheryl's Action Plan

Problem-focused coping strategies will motivate Cheryl and influence her recovery by setting and working toward long-term and short-term goals, thus establishing realistic daily goals that serve to enhance her confidence. This strategy will start with a *re-appraisal* of the negative life event. This will facilitate the actual application of problem-based coping, increasing understanding by means of personal reflection, in addition to seeking social support, and positive feedback. This approach leads to a constructive plan of action, thereby subsequently executing the proposed plan.

Emotion- and problem-based coping serve to strengthen and empower athletes such as Cheryl with numerous perceived positive outcomes. By utilizing both methods, the key issue is being addressed: Cheryl's stress level regarding her injury. This point is worth reiterating. As previously stated, an athlete's ability to adhere to their rehabilitation program is the number one factor affecting successful rehabilitation outcomes. Through the use of emotion- and problem-based coping strategies, Cheryl can greatly reduce her stress level and regain her confidence while serving as a role model to others. Through this reappraisal of negative life events, Cheryl is able to reconnect with her motivational spirit.

Remember:

An individual's perception of their level of confidence and degree of control are strong interactive variables that influence rehabilitation adherence. Other factors include attitude in general, perception toward rehabilitation team, its process, and belief in a successful rehabilitation outcome. Perhaps one of the most significant psychological factors that affect a person's adherence to their rehabilitation program is their level of motivation.

Closing Thoughts

Over time, chronic *sleep deprivation* can cause a wide range of health problems, including increased levels of stress hormones, anxiety, and memory problems; therefore, everyone should make getting a quality night's sleep a daily goal.

Remember, our thoughts (positive or negative) impact our emotions, thus affecting our stress levels and subsequent response to stressors. In essence, much of our stress response is a product of our inner self-dialogue, the thoughts that either increase or reduce stress and anxiety levels. This is why I consider *positive thinking* the foundation of human motivation because without it, stress increases, enjoyment decreases, and goals and dreams are not realized.

Chapter 6

Activation and Relaxation:
Two Necessary Tools to Regulate Motivation

Where do you use energizing techniques?

The simple answer is wherever you need to in order to increase energy for those important moments that require energy. As it pertains to athletes, this means that energizing techniques can be used just about anywhere from on the bus in route to the game, to the locker room right before tip-off, or even within the game itself. Also, everyday tasks often present the need for us to feel an increased level of energy, especially when they become less than exciting.

Self-Reflection Exercise:

What are some occasions that you need to energize? Reflect back to your own performances: what are the times where you had low energy levels? Currently, in what moments would more energy be valuable to you?

Think of an energizing cue that you can use in the upcoming week. It can be an image, word, acronym, or phrase. Choose 3 opportunities to use the cue immediately prior to a challenge or event in which you need an extra boost of energy.

Description of My Own Experiences with This Exercise

The 3 opportunities to utilize cue words prior to a challenge were before and during 3 previous workouts. I said the phrase, "This is going to be a great workout," several times while driving to the gym. This positive phrase help set the tone for the workouts. Also, before doing an exercise or a new set, I said to myself, "Go!" and "Push it!" I utilized these energizing cue words more often as the challenge of the workouts increased, especially during the 3rd workout. In combination with music, the cue words definitely helped me feel more energized and looking forward to each repetition. The words were like a symbolic green light to Go! as in a race, beginning each rep with full attention and engagement.

5 Contributing Factors to Over-Arousal:

1) A negative appraisal/perspective of the situation, doubting one's ability
2) Uncertainty, often derived from low confidence levels
3) Increased expectations, often derived from an outcome orientation, a focus on winning and rewards
4) Environmental factors, such as having to play a football game on a windy, rainy day
5) Anxiety: Possessing a predisposition to become anxious and over aroused

Why are Relaxation Skills a Valuable Tool for You?

The answer is, quite often, as human beings, we develop a particular pattern of over-activation, rooted in anxiety and worry about our ability to complete the task at hand. Learning to relax is fundamental in regulating these negative responses to avoid any damaging effects on performance.

In pursuit to learn to avoid too much tension you must recognize tension and to relax and release the unwanted tension. Such awareness increases your sensitivity to tension levels and your ability to regulate varying levels of tension to equal the demands of the performance situation. The ability to completely relax provides you with the foundation for learning the skill of momentary relaxation, which can be used quickly. It does not accomplish as deep of a relaxation state as complete relaxation. However, momentary relaxation skills are very important for you because they can be used to reduce over-activation, being too hyped up at any given point during practice, competition, or work.

Muscle to Mind & Mind to Muscle Relaxation Techniques: [1] Both approaches are effective; the point is to disrupt the stimulus-response pattern of half of the nerves leading to the brain or away from the brain. Learning to reduce the sensation in either half of the circuit will interrupt the stimulation necessary to produce unwanted muscular tension.

Muscle to Mind Techniques: Breathing exercises and progressive relaxation techniques fall into this category.

3 Breathing Exercises

1) Complete Breathing
With a complete breath (also referred to as a circle breath), the diaphragm fills down causing the stomach to expand and a vacuum happens in the lungs, thus filling the lungs up from the bottom. Whenever you get too tense, you should attempt to recreate the calmness prompted by practicing this exercise. After you have learned the process of complete breathing, you should take approximately 30 to 40 deep breaths each day: this serves as a good example of a daily goal, as discussed in Chapter 3 on goal setting.

2) Concentration Breathing
This allows you, especially athletes, to focus your attention on your *breathing rhythm*. If your mind wanders to some distracting thought

between inhaling and exhaling, (for example, thinking about what you are having for lunch, etc.) concentration breathing redirects attention back to your next breath, allowing the intruding thought to disappear. The goal is to think of becoming more relaxed with each exhalation as you continue to focus on the *rhythm* of your breathing. This is a great exercise for athletes to practice when they are having distracting thoughts, during practice and athletic competition.

3) Rhythmic Breathing
This entails inhaling to a count of 4, holding for a count of 4, exhaling to a count of 4, and pausing for a count of 4 before repeating the sequence 3-5 times. This exercise is especially useful for athletes to utilize before competition.

4 Progressive Relaxation Techniques
The objective of progressive relaxation is to train the muscles to become sensitive to any level of tension and to be able to release that tension.

1) Specific Progressive Relaxation
This technique involves a series of exercises that entail contracting a specific muscle group, holding the contraction for 5-7 seconds, then relaxing. The exercises progress from one muscle group to another. The contraction phase teaches you awareness of what muscular tension feels like. The releasing of muscular tension, or relaxation phase, teaches an awareness of what the absence of tension feels like and that it can be brought about by releasing the tension in a muscle.

2) Active Relaxation
The goal of this exercise is to spot the tension and release it *before* it leads to backaches and headaches, or performance concerns. Signs that point to difficulty relaxing include darting eyes, frowning, rapid breathing, and fidgeting.

3) Quick Body Scan

This technique is very beneficial for *momentary* muscle relaxation; it is great for use during performance, such as just before serving in tennis, shooting a free throw in basketball, pitching in baseball, or even while running, particularly in the middle of long-distance runs. You can quickly scan the body from head to toe (or toe to head). Stop only at muscle groups where the tension level is too high. Release the tension and continue the scan down (or up) the body.

4) Sport Muscle Check

This momentary scan checks whatever muscle group is most suitable for the sport skill being utilized. For example, batters could squeeze their bat and golfers their golf club followed by relaxing to the proper level.

3 Mind to Muscle Relaxation Techniques

1) Meditation Practice

The foundational pieces that are common to most types of meditation are a quiet environment, a relaxed position, and a mental device such as a mantra or fixed gazing at an object. Such elements assist in quieting the mind by providing a *focus* of attention on something that is nonarousing, nondistracting, nonstimulating, and free of worry.

2) Autogenic Training

This training involves a series of exercises intended to produce 2 physical sensations usually associated with relaxation—*warmth* and *heaviness*. It is a technique of autohypnosis or self-hypnosis. The goal here is for you to focus your attention on the sensations you are trying to produce. As in meditation, it is essential to just let the feeling happen in a very passive manner.

It typically requires several months of 10-30 minutes of daily practice, hence lots of dedication to become skilled using this technique. Although this exercise involves a lot of time and effort, it is worth trying because some people find this exercise to be very beneficial in their efforts to relax.

The 5-Step Autogenic Training Sequence in Practice

Repeat the following:

1) "My arms and legs are heavy" a total of six times; "I am calm" once.
2) "My arms and legs feel warm" six times; "I am calm" once.
3) "My heartbeat is calm and regular" six times; "Calm" once.
4) "Sun rays are streaming warm and quiet" six times, repeat the word "calm" once.
5) "My forehead feels cool" six times, "Calm" once.

3) Imagery Practice

Imagery skills, being able to visualize being in a place favorable to relaxation, is another successful technique for eliciting relaxation. Whatever image that provides you with a sense of calm and relaxation is the one you should use. Please refer to Chapter 10 on Imagery for further information on the benefits of consistent imagery practice.

Consistent Practice Is Vital When Practicing Relaxation Techniques

Relaxation skills must be practiced on a *consistent* basis, just like learning any new sport or task. When learning relaxation techniques, it is more effective to start training after a workout or a long day at work, for example, because it is easier to relax muscular tension when you are physically fatigued. Keep in mind, relaxation techniques tend to lower anxiety and tension in general, and most people typically show improvement within a week or two of consistent practice. Also keep in mind that consistently practicing relaxation techniques is another great daily goal that has the added benefit of becoming a positive habit.

Closing Thought

The human nervous system is ultimately responsible for effective movement and execution of various tasks; it is the origin and essence of human movement. Therefore, accurate activation and relaxation of the nervous system are essential tools to optimal task completion and motivation regulation.

Chapter 7

Focus and Concentration:
Zeroing In on Our Goals

"Concentration is the secret of strength." – Ralph Waldo Emerson

"At any given time, our senses detect information from millions of sources: images through our eyes, aromas through our olfactory organs, sounds through our ears, pressure applied to our skin, the position of our body in space, and the myriad of thoughts and emotions that flash through our brains. How do we filter out the information that is vital to success from that which is useless? The question has plagued cognitive scientists, sport psychologists, coaches, and athletes for decades, or in the case of Aristotle and Plato, pondering for centuries."[1]

Action Components for Achieving our Goals

Focusing and refocusing are critical action components for learning, performing, and achieving our goals. We as individuals and teams cannot perform consistently close to our potential without these skills. Effective focusing, and effective refocusing, are essential tools for elite athletes, coaches, students, business executives, and performers in all disciplines because these skills are indispensable for *consistent* high-level performance.

Individuals who consistently perform close or up to their potential have learned to do **3** things successfully: **1**) direct and connect their focus, **2**) direct their emotions in positive directions, and **3**) bounce back from setbacks quickly and effectively. Elite athletes have refined their ability to focus completely on what they are engaged in. If the need arises, they can shift focus from negative to positive, particularly in response to anxiety, big challenges, errors, self-doubts, or setbacks. [2] When you learn to do this, your odds of getting the most out of your preparation and the best out of yourself when it really counts most will increase significantly. You can perform your best on a consistent basis by developing the focusing skills required to excel. By finding and keeping a positive, connected focus that works for you, over the duration of your life or career you will refine and improve the focus that cultivates your best performances.

Zeroing In on the Task at Hand

Maximally demanding conditions and solid concentration involve 100% attention on the task at hand. The major element of concentration is the ability to selectively attend to appropriate cues while eliminating distracting and irrelevant internal and external stimuli. Concentration is essentially being able to focus *when* and *how* you want to execute a particular task, based on the given demands of the task that you are doing.

Given that there is so much that you could pay attention to and so many things that could pull your focus away from the task at hand, it is essential that you learn how to improve your concentration and focus skills, as well as being able to improve your ability to refocus when needed.

Why Do We Lose Focus?

To perform at our best, focusing on the present moment is necessary. However, it is very easy to think back about what has already occurred or look forward to what we want to happen or wish to avoid. Focus can be lost if an individual does not have the ability to apply their concentration in the manner that their sport or the task at hand demands. The capability to maintain and shift focus does not come naturally to everyone; fortunately, you can learn by gaining awareness and consistent practice.

When Do We Lose Focus?

After a basketball player misses a free throw, he may be thinking about this mistake and then find himself distracted the next time the ball is passed to him. Pressure or stress often facilitates a loss of focus. For example, if a high school baseball player is up at the bottom of the 9th, and the outcome of the game depends on how he does, he might become focused on irrelevant factors such as wanting to look impressive. When an athlete lacks motivation or is over-motivated, this can cause the mind to wonder. If skills possessed do not match up with the skills required to complete the task—for example, if an athlete feels that a particular task is beyond their abilities—motivation will be lacking, and subsequently their focus will decrease.

Understanding Distractions

Athletes can be distracted by a multitude of things; these distractions usually fall into 2 categories: internal and external distractions.

Internal distractions are feelings, thoughts, body sensations, mood state, pain, rapid heart rate, which serve to pull your attention away from focusing on the task at hand.

External distractions include crowd behavior, weather conditions, referee calls, friends and family in the stands, and behavior of opposing team. These all have the potential to greatly impact your ability to dedicate 100% of your concentration to the task at hand.

Consider the following questions:

What distractions do you face in your sport participation or everyday life? Are you more likely to be distracted by internal or external distractions? What impact do these distractions have on your performance?

2 Types of Focus: Direction and Width

1) **Direction**
Direction of focus is whether your focus is directed internally or externally. Each sport will have specific demands of attention; athletes need to have the ability to focus both internally as well as externally. For example, a golfer may mentally analyze her shot (inward direction of focus) and then proceed to shift focus externally to executing the shot.

2) **Width**
Width of focus involves how wide or how narrow your focus is. For instance, every sport has specific demands connected to the width of your attention; it is likely athletes will need to shift how wide their focus is. A quarterback would use a broad focus to scan the field and determine the best option, and then would shift to a narrow focus to throw to the open receiver.

4 General Types of Focus Style:

1) **Broad-External:** Concentration is on a wide range of cues outside of oneself; for example, basketball point guards and soccer players in general typically must possess this type of focus to be successful.

2) **Broad-Internal:** This style engages in a considerable amount of analysis and problem-solving during competition; for example, chess players and golfers.

3) **Narrow-External:** This focus style directs attention to a limited number of cues outside of the athlete that are essential to optimal

performance; for example, pitchers in baseball usually need a narrow-external focus style.

4) **Narrow-Internal**: The focus here is on one's ability to focus just on 1 or 2 internal cues. This type of narrow focus helps athletes block out distractions and is typically used in such sports as weightlifting and sprinting. Importantly noted, it is possible to need to engage in all four types of attention at different points, during performance.

Remember:

It is critical to understand how to shift focus from one focus style to the next. For example, if a golfer needs to shift from analyzing to performing, only to find him or herself stuck in the thinking phase (broad internal), and is unable to move to the swing phase, then optimal performance is out of reach.

3 Strategies for Athletes to Address External Distractions

1) **Dress Rehearsal:** By practicing in competition uniforms outside of the competition setting, athletes have the opportunity to get comfortable and adjust to their uniforms, and therefore they are less likely to be distracted in the actual competition. For example, in figure skating, competition costumes are often quite different from their training gear.

2) **Simulation Training**: This technique simply involves making practice as real as an actual competition as possible. By practicing dealing with pressure and maintaining an appropriate focus through simulation of pressure situations, an athlete is better equipped to handle the situation when it really happens. An example of this occurs in the NFL, where teams anticipating a great deal of crowd noise in their upcoming game will practice while being blasted by loud recordings.

3) **Imagery Rehearsal:** Athletes can utilize this amazing psychological tool to practice dealing with distractions as they occur. For example, athletes can picture themselves faced with distractions and having an appropriate focus, as well as refocusing when the moment calls for it, such as a gymnast going to a new sporting environment with unfamiliar surroundings and stimuli.

3 Strategies for Managing Internal Distractions

When dealing with internal distractions, verbal cues or physical or visual triggers can prompt you to appropriately focus or regain focus after a distraction.

1) **Verbal cues** are powerful tools that you can use to achieve optimal focus. Cue words help to establish proper focus *prior* to a competition and may also be utilized *throughout* the competition to maintain focus. Examples include "focus, swing, smooth, etc." A great way to develop a verbal cue word is to develop a *process focus*, focusing on the *how* of performing optimally. Verbal cues are essentially *reminders* as to *where* your focus should be, and if you are focusing appropriately.

2) **Physical triggers** are physical actions that remind you to focus; for example, a tennis player tapping their leg with their racquet in an effort to focus.

3) **Visual triggers** are places that you can look to in order to focus or regain focus; for example, something stationary (far end of swimming pool), not something that can move like another athlete.

A Process-Directed Focus

Attaining a *process focus* can be extremely efficient in enhancing athletic performance. Turning your attention toward losing or winning rarely helps your athletic success. If athletes are focused on performance outcomes, they are not focused on *cues* relevant to performing well; therefore, an outcome focus actually diminishes performance. As an athlete, ask yourself, "What do I need to do *right now* to focus on the task at hand, to perform at my best?" Answering this question will take your focus away from dwelling on past errors or focusing on future results and will bring your attention to what you can *control*, the present moment!

Remember:

The ability to focus is being able to concentrate *when* and *how* you want to perform a particular task, based on the given demands of the task you are engaged in.

3 Focusing Errors

1) The first type of error happens when focus is *too broad*; attention is not focused on the necessary elements for successful task completion.

2) The second type of error happens when focus is pointed in the *wrong direction* altogether. In this instance, attention is distracted by irrelevant information. An example of this type of error in golf occurs when a golfer maintains awareness of a double bogey on the previous hole while attempting a swing on the current hole. The knowledge of scoring a double bogey on the previous hole is not relevant to the mental and physical skills necessary to perform the current swing.

3) The third type of error happens when focus is *too narrow* or moves too slowly. In this instance, attention is not divided efficiently, nor does not take into consideration all the necessary stimuli.

4 Focusing Exercises

1) Broad-External Exercise
Look straight in front of you, seeing as much of the room that you are in as possible, in addition to as many objects in the room as your

peripheral vision will permit. The goal is to observe the entire room, and all of the various items in it.

2) Broad-Internal Exercise

The goal is to focus your attention on all body sensations that you are experiencing while simultaneously attending to what you are thinking and feeling. It is important that you remain passive, maintaining an open awareness. Repeat this exercise, except this time, do it when performing in a high-stress environment. Then contrast these two experiences; this will help you *identify* the subtle changes that sometimes happen in high-stress situations that can lead to inadequate performance.

3) Narrow-External Exercise

Choose an object across the room and focus in on it. You should make a point to observe every detail of the object, not just simply noticing it. Once there is nothing else to observe, focus your attention on a different object. Now, proceed to pay attention to what you hear by identifying each sound and mentally labeling it; for example, someone's voice. Importantly, focus on only *one* sound at a time.

4) Narrow-Internal Exercise

First, take 3-5 breaths. As you inhale, feel the air coming in, pause, then let the air naturally come out for a longer time than it took to inhale. Next, redirect your attention to any muscle group, taking notice to any tension that you are feeling, and if you can release this tension, contrast the feeling. Then, focus on only *one* emotion or thought; identify its nature. Remain calm and relaxed, allowing yourself to feel one thought and then *effortlessly* move to another. The ultimate goal is to "tune-in" to one thought or emotion and hold your focus there, hence the narrow-internal focus style.

Focusing & Distraction Facts

Our attention is often easily distracted; thus, we lose our focus. Distractions deplete the prefrontal cortex's limited resources. For example, being "always on," being connected to others via technology, can lower your IQ dramatically, as much as losing an entire night's sleep." [3]

The fact is, you can focus on only 1 conscious task at a time with full concentration. If you perform multiple conscious tasks at once you will experience a significant drop in performance and information retention. The only way to perform 2 mental tasks quickly, if accuracy is vital, is doing 1 of them at a time. Switching between tasks utilizes energy; if you do this a lot, your chances for making mistakes increases.[3]

Refocusing Reminders:

Effective refocusing reminders in potentially stressful situations often start with a reminder to breathe. Focus reminders include: "breathe, relax, focus, focus, focus, decide, decide, act, act." "Change the channel. I control my focus; it's my choice. Be totally here. Be in the moment"

Only 1 or 2 simple but powerful reminders are needed when you need to stay in control or to regain control. Keep in mind that the "control switch" always resides within you! Make the choice to flip the switch. The next time that something distracts you—too much thinking, a negative comment, a missed move—challenge yourself to turn it around within that environment.

Case Study Example: Michael

Michael is a seventeen-year-old track and field athlete. His areas of specialization include sprints and the 100- and 200-meter races. One of his primary goals is to earn a track scholarship that will allow him to attend college. Coach Myers shares with me that he feels Michael has been losing his focus. He allows noise in the stadium to bother him, subsequently letting the other runners make him hesitant, and he is definitely worried about receiving a scholarship. "It seems that I am unable to talk any sense into him, and these lapses in concentration are slowing him down, restricting his potential and overall growth as an athlete."

Michael states that lately all he has been able to focus on is the coach's negative comments. When he is getting ready for the 100, all he can think about is Coach Myers saying what not to do: "Don't look at the runner next to you, Michael," or "Don't be slow out of the blocks!" Michael attempts to shift his focus, but his thoughts just stress him out. "I feel like I have a million thoughts racing through my head, and very few of them have to do with me running my race."

Michael really wants to train with the running club this summer but is unsure if his family can afford it. He says, "The club is very expensive, but I need to train there to have a chance of getting noticed and earning a scholarship." Michael feels bad about having to ask his parents for the money, and so this is a cause of stress and worry for him. Michael goes on to say, "I feel a lot of pressure to train with the running club because I will not be able to go to a four-year school unless I earn a scholarship."

Michael has a big track meet next Friday, and Coach Myers has informed him that college scouts will be there seeking "rising stars" with obvious talent. Michael tells me he feels anxious and that he will not perform well.

Assessing Michael's Situation

Michael's beliefs serve to facilitate what he *expects* to happen; such beliefs can potentially cause stress and anxiety. For example, Michael believes that he needs to train at an expensive club. He also says that he feels nervous and anxious and believes he won't perform well. He is exhibiting negative self-dialogue in the form of hearing nothing but Coach Myer's negative comments. Michael's negative thoughts are affecting how he feels, and subsequently influencing his behavior as displayed in his inability to focus.

In efforts to assist Michael regain the necessary focus, the following questions are addressed: "Can you recall a past <u>peak</u> performance, in efforts to identify what shifts in focus happened, in addition to the amount of focus required?" "Do you notice a difference in your energy levels in practice compared to competition? If so, can you expand on this?" "Do you have a good understanding of the moments in which you need to be highly focused?" "Are you clear on *what* to focus on?" "What are your expectations? Are they under your control?" "Are these expectations coming from you or other people?" "What are these beliefs based upon? Are they helpful to you?"

Creating a Plan for Michael

The two primary strategies that Michael should utilize are *cues* and *triggers*. A cue word, such as *stop* will remind Michael to focus. A great way for Michael to make use of a cue word is to develop a *process focus*, focusing on the *how* of performing optimally. He should use self-dialogue by asking himself, "*What* do I need to do in order to perform at my best?" A trigger is recommended in the form of a *visual cue*, consisting of a mental image of a stop sign in connection with a self-dialogue cue.

I also recommend *concentration breathing*; this is excellent for redirecting focus back to the task at hand. The best time for Michael to utilize these strategies is in preparation for the 100; this is when he is having the most difficulty focusing. Michael can utilize these strategies before, during, and after competition, whenever negative self-dialogue is present.

Centering: Staying focused and grounded
What is the Practice of Centering?

Centering is an exercise of focused attention, concentrating on "one point" as a way of gaining control over tension and a loss of focus in pressure-provoking situations. This one point represents the center of gravity; it is below and behind the navel. The essence of centering is about feeling in control, confident, and grounded. It involves a combination of skills, including breathing and focusing. It is a conscious process, not something achieved automatically.

Benefits of Centering

Once centered, you will feel increased stability, strength, and confidence. By centering, you will be able to control concentration and tension in your performance, especially during high-pressure situations. Centering assists in facilitating appropriate breathing, regulating arousal levels, and directing attention and optimal focus to the task at hand. A distinctive benefit of centering is the feeling of increased stability.

When to Practice Centering

Centering is beneficial to you in an out of your athletic performances because it assists you in starting from a *consistent* place. This is great to utilize for practice, competition, as well as everyday life.

Sometimes athletes feel that centering can only be performed during breaks in performance; however, if an athlete possesses the ability to focus on centering, it can be done while performing. This is a more advanced centering method, and you should feel comfortable centering outside of performance first. You will take more ownership if you come up with the ways to use centering in your sport. Once you learn this skill, you should brainstorm times where centering is possible and best for your sport. The timing for centering is different for all sports.

Centering is especially needed when confidence is lacking, performance expectancies are high, when angry, anxious, frustrated, worried, and when focus mistakes are more likely to happen.

Importantly noted, when centering immediately before your activity, be sure to go directly to the task at hand because any time between centering and the activity might allow distractions to enter into your awareness.

The First Step to Athletic Success

Centering is the first step to assist you in being fully engaged and prepared for your athletic performance. Centering can be thought of as a "reset button," as it allows you to take a moment and consistently get back to a confident, solid, focused place where your energy level is under *control*. Thinking of centering in this fashion might also assist you in determining appropriate times to center in sport and/or everyday life.

The reason that breathing and muscle tension get out of control during sports participation is that most athletes do not take the time to pay attention to their bodies. When under pressure, we stop thinking. As a result, we become aware of the tension after it is too late, often after performance has been negatively impacted. Importantly noted, taking the time to mentally check and to adjust your breathing and muscle tension prompts a conscious effort of attending to your breathing. This has a secondary effect; it is not possible to consciously focus on both breathing and worrisome thoughts!

Your goal when centering is to accomplish the necessary momentary clearing and readjustment that maximizes the likelihood that you will be able to zero in on the task at hand. Essentially, you are establishing and providing a base from which to initiate activity. The development of this base will lead to *consistency*, in your athletic performances. If you always begin at the same place, you are much more likely to be consistent whether you are swinging a baseball bat, golf club, a tennis racquet, or approaching a performance as a gymnast.

Additional Benefits of Centering

Many athletes use centering as a momentary time-out, a reminder to slow down and/or to analyze *before* reacting to their sporting situation, thus taking a proactive stance as opposed to simply reacting without preparation.

Question for You to Think About:

What have been some instances where you found yourself pressured to respond *before* you were ready?

The 3-Step Centering Process

1) Stand with your feet approximately shoulder distance apart, with 1 foot slightly in front of the other and knees slightly bent. Try to achieve a position of the greatest stability. Begin by inhaling and exhaling deeply (3-4 deep breaths).

2) While slowly inhaling deeply, mentally check the tension in your neck, shoulders, and chest and proceed to consciously let them relax.

3) While exhaling, relax the muscles in your calves and thighs and let your hips drop lower. At this point, you should feel an increased heaviness and a greater contact with the ground as you slightly lower your weight. At the end of your exhale, you are now ready to redirect attention to the task at hand.

3 Key Points to Remember

1) When first learning the skill of centering, it might take several minutes to feel completely centered. Eventually, with *consistent* practice, you can likely feel centered in just 1 or 2 breaths.

2) It is best to begin training from a standing position because most sports and physical activity are done standing, and this is a more challenging position than sitting. Therefore, if you can center from this position, you will more likely be able to center from other positions more easily.

3) Remember, centering is a *conscious* process. If you can obtain similar feelings automatically, then this is not true centering. Part of the "how" of this skill is having an appropriate focus immediately following the centering process.

6 Sport-Specific Examples of Ideal Times to Practice Centering

1) As a baseball pitcher, just after receiving the catcher's sign and selection of a pitch.
2) As a defensive football player, just as the quarterback steps up to the center.
3) As a football receiver, when running a passing route, just before making a cut in your route.
4) As a punter, when punting, just prior to the snap.
5) As a golfer, immediately after you have mentally practiced a shot.
6) As a gymnast, immediately prior to the execution of a tumbling routine.

Closing Thoughts

As previously mentioned, centering is the 1st step to assist you in being fully engaged and prepared for your athletic performance or the task at hand. Remember, centering can be thought of as a "reset button," as it allows you to take a moment to get back to a confident, solid, focused place, grounded and ready for a challenge.

Set goals to reestablish your positive focus and total connection with your performance as soon as possible. Refocusing in a constructive fashion is quite often a challenge. However, when you are successful at keeping track of *what* you focused on to achieve success, this will help you reach your goals and keep your motivational spirit solid as a rock!

Chapter 8

Self-Dialogue:
Our Internal Voice That Directs Our Motivational Spirit

Self-talk is the dialogue that we have with ourselves. It can consist of the following: our internal voice that no one else hears, mumbling, as well as thoughts that are expressed out loud. Self-talk can be about ourselves, a particular situation, or other people. Typically, self-dialogue is categorized as either positive, negative, or neutral.

In a sporting context, John, a tennis player, might have positive thoughts such as, "I am ready; I am quick." Negative thoughts may include, "This guy is very good; he knows how to counter all of my moves." Importantly noted, negative thoughts can also be thoughts that are not useful in the context of the situation, and therefore create a distraction. For example, if Carlos, a baseball player, is thinking about all of the things he has to do when he's finished with the game, this might not be negative in the sense that he is getting down on himself, but it is *not* beneficial to the situation. Neutral thoughts are those that are not necessarily positive or negative, and do not seem to have much significance for the individual in a positive or negative fashion.

It is important to examine and understand what you believe about yourself and your surroundings—positive/negative, rational/irrational—because these beliefs lead to what you expect to happen. Such beliefs have the potential to produce position thoughts, or stress and anxiety. Our thoughts greatly influence performance, so our self-dialogue and confidence become very much intertwined. Additionally, confidence develops over time, and develops not only from having success but also from thinking positively and effectively.

Keys to Success

In order to change our thoughts, we must first become aware of them and their source. *Awareness* is essential because our thoughts have the potential to greatly influence our actions.

In addition to managing negative self-dialogue and self-doubt, individuals need to realize that they might also be engaging in cognitive distortions, as well as irrational thinking. According to Ellis (1982),[1] "Athletes fail to reach their goals and perform below their ability primarily because they accept and endorse self-defeating, irrational beliefs." Obviously, this type of thinking is counterproductive because it decreases motivation.

3 Methods for Building Awareness of Your Thoughts

1) Self-talk log
Logs or journals can be helpful because information is captured shortly after the thoughts happen. Write down the situation that leads to the thought and any impact on your performance.

2) Tape recorder
A digital recorder (or phone) can be conveniently used to capture thoughts at specific moments.

3) Review video
Watch and review a previous athletic/exercise performance and recall what you were thinking at specific moments, in addition to reflecting/observing how your performance was impacted by those thoughts.

3 Strategies for Acquiring Positive Self-Dialogue

1) Countering

This strategy challenges negative self-dialogue using *logic* and *facts* to assist you in believing that the opposite of the initial negative thought is true.

When using this method, you need to describe the evidence necessary to change a belief. What is key here is determining whether a specified thought helps you reach your goal. Ask yourself, "Is this self-dialogue beneficial to me?" "Does this thinking assist me in feeling the way I want, or does it cause me to worry?" "Does this self-talk assist me in performing better?" When you truly realize that thinking certain thoughts is detrimental, it then becomes sensible, and therefore easier, to change them or eliminate them.

2) Reframing

Reframing occurs when we make the conscious effort to look at a situation from a different point of view because, as we know, there is always a different perspective when it comes to evaluating situations or events.

It is the process of creating different ways at looking at the world because the world is literally what we make it. Reframing permits you to transform what appears at first to be a weakness or difficulty into a strength or a real possibility, simply by looking at it from a different perspective. Almost any negative thought can be reframed or understood from a different point of view, so that it helps you rather than hindering your progress and enjoyment of life.

A significant element of reframing is that it does not deny or downplay what you are experiencing or encourage you to ignore something troublesome. Instead, by reframing, you acknowledge what is occurring and decide to utilize it to your best advantage. For example, if a high school basketball player states, "I'm feeling anxious and tense about playing today," he or she can reframe the statement to "I'm feeling excited and ready!" Similarly, a basketball player dwelling on such problems as improving skills or the struggle of a performance slump can turn these challenges to his or her advantage and maintain a positive attitude by directing focus to the possibility of achieving a new level of skill and the opportunity to learn something from each and every performance.

3) The ABC Approach [2]

This strategy utilizes a 3-step process to change irrational thinking and distorted self-dialog. For instance, Steve, a college basketball player, misses a crucial free throw in the final ten seconds of a playoff game and ends up feeling defeated and fearing similar situations in the future. Steve most likely thinks his missed free throw facilitated counterproductive thoughts and anxiety. However, the *assumptions* that he made are the foundational cause. In this instance, irrational expectations such as perfectionism, one's worth depends on achievement, or perhaps personalization may be a factor.

The goal here is to get Steve to identify and dispute his irrational assumptions, thus decreasing his self-caused pressure. An excellent means to accomplish this goal is to utilize Albert Ellis's rational emotive therapy method, also referred to as ABC cognitive restructuring. The process starts by getting Steve to keep a daily record in which he records not only his upsetting thoughts but also the resulting feelings and behavior, in addition to the negative events that prompted them. In column **A** he should briefly describe the situation in terms of what occurred, what he saw and heard. In column **B** he should record the exact content of his dysfunctional self-dialogue; that is, whatever he thought or said out loud that could be interpreted as counterproductive. In column **C** he is to record the resulting behavioral and emotional consequences. The following 5 questions will help Steve determine what he should record:

1) Are my beliefs grounded in objective reality?

2) Would a diverse group of people all agree that the situation occurred the way I perceived it, or do I exaggerate and personalize such experiences?

3) Are these beliefs and thoughts beneficial to me? (Self-destructive thoughts are typically irrational.)
4) Do my thoughts assist me in reaching my short- and long-term goals, or do they inhibit my success?
5) Do my thoughts decrease emotional conflict and assist me in feeling the way I want to feel?

After having completed the ABC steps over a predetermined number of days, the next step involves Steve trying to dispute his self-criticism. *First,* he needs to reexamine the self-dialogue under column B to determine the distortions in thinking or irrational self-dialogue that may underlie what appeared to be automatic counterproductive statements. In many instances, more than one thinking error might have led to his self-dialogue.

Recognizing the underlying irrational beliefs and thinking distortions will assist Steve in discovering the mistaken or illogical aspects of his initial self-dialogue. Once this task is accomplished, he is ready to substitute more productive thoughts. If a certain dysfunctional thought often happens (e.g. saying, "Most of the time, I screw up," or something comparable after every such disappointment), he will need to frequently repeat the substituted rational statement until it is fully believed. Incorporating a quick relaxation technique prior to saying the statement might increase the likelihood of believing the statement. For instance, he takes a deep breath and with the exhalation says, "Even the best athletes make mistakes, the important thing is to learn from it and move on…now focus on the task at hand." The proceeding task might be challenging, but the good news is that it gets easier and easier with *consistent* practice.

The foundational goal here is to create such awareness in Steve that when he recognizes his own dysfunctional self-dialogue, he *immediately* disputes it. If he reflects back to his best performances in competition, he will be more in line with the positive thoughts that served him well. By eliminating his irrational beliefs and developing more adaptive, productive self-dialogue, Steve will go a long way toward improving his performance and, perhaps more significantly, strengthening his motivational spirit!

4 Uses for Positive Self-Dialogue

1) Skill Building

Athletes, for example, quite often think while performing, though some may not be aware of the thoughts they have. When learning a skill, athletes can give themselves instructional cue words that help them focus on the appropriate parts of the skill execution. The athlete needs to break down the skill, keeping the cues short and simple, but also be aware that different sports will likely require different kinds of self-dialogue and at different times. As an athlete's skill level changes, so will his or her self-dialogue. Over time, skills will become more automatic, and so the cues might be used less often.

2) Changing Bad Habits

You can use self-dialogue to help stay motivated when changing habits and giving yourself reminders as needed, remembering to focus on the positives and planning what to say so that you are focusing on what you want to have happen instead of what you are trying to avoid.

3) Focus Control

Many of the strategies for controlling self-dialogue are very similar to those to control focus. Since focus and self-dialogue are both mental processes, similar cognitive techniques are beneficial. You can select self-dialogue cues that help you to stay in the moment and focused on the task at hand.

4) Emotional Creation and Control

Self-dialogue can assist you in creating a specific effect or mood, as well as helping to control emotions. Words or phrases that specifically address emotion can be utilized to help you control or change the way you are feeling. For example, words or phrases such as *calm, collected, relaxed, in control, powerful,* etc. can create certain feelings for you and create or change mood or energy as needed.

Case Study Example: Jerry

Jerry is a sixteen-year-old horseback rider (jumper rider). He has 3 horses and shows about 15 to 18 weeks a year. His father, Randy, who is also one of his trainers, referred Jerry to me. Randy states: "Jerry isn't really having fun anymore. He gets very nervous and stressed; it's like the shows are becoming rather torturous for him. We have never pushed Jerry to ride horses and compete, and we have no plans of doing so."

Jerry feels like everybody works especially hard and contributes so much time into helping him that he will let them down if he doesn't perform well. He states: "The expenses are enormous. I do ride well; therefore, there really isn't any reason I shouldn't be perfect. Elizabeth (Jerry's other trainer) has always had somebody win one of the national finals, and now that she offered to assist me in developing my jumper rider skills, I definitely do not want to let her down…that's for sure!"

Jerry gets flustered and nervous prior to going into the ring. He tells me his stomach gets "twisted in knots at the bigger shows in Kentucky." He gets nervous when friends and other riders say things such as: "You've got this, for sure," "You'll win, Jerry," "You're zoned in, today…you're the man!" These "encouragements" stay with Jerry and make him feel stressed as he replays them over and over in his mind.

When I began to facilitate him writing affirmations, he writes, "Everybody has faith in me," and "We are a team." Although, Jerry is nervous and stressed, he is also very serious about improving his riding skills and has a long-term goal of competing in the Olympics.

Addressing Jerry's Concerns

Athletes such as Jerry may not realize that they have *control* over their beliefs, expectations, self-dialogue, and actions; however, with help they can take the necessary steps to take control over how they think, feel, and perform. Jerry's self-dialogue establishes a foundation for formulating irrational/rational, positive, or negative beliefs; these lead to what he expects to happen. His thoughts are influencing his feelings, which in turn affect his behavior. For example, Jerry's friends provide "encouragements," such as, "You'll win for sure, Jerry." This creates *expectations* solely focusing on an outcome goal. This then leads to Jerry feeling nervous, flustered, less focused, and stressed.

In efforts to gain an *understanding* of how Jerry attributes his beliefs, I address the following questions with Jerry: "What would occur if you did not perform well?" "What fears does not doing well elicit?" "Do you think your beliefs are *beneficial* to you?" "Are your expectations and related goals realistic?" "Are these expectations based upon things you can *control*, or are they derived from other people? "How confident are you, on a scale of 1-10, in reaching your goal(s)?"

After Jerry understands how negative self-dialogue affects his expectations, he will utilize **retrospection**, which involves Jerry thinking back to prior successful experiences *without* stressful expectations. A **self-talk log** is also recommended because his negative thoughts can be captured, either written down or recorded via a recorder or phone. Subsequently, Jerry's irrational beliefs and self-dialogue need to be recognized and disputed (for example, his belief that he must perform perfectly). Upon recognizing his counterproductive beliefs in regard to perfectionism, Jerry's internal voice will be telling him to strive for excellence and to continually seek new ways to improve his skills as a jumper rider.

Closing Thought

Our thoughts impact our feelings, and our feelings subsequently have the capacity to greatly affect our behavior. Positive self-dialogue is truly the foundation of finding, fueling, and keeping your motivational spirit solid as a rock!

Chapter 9

Positive Thinking:
The Foundation of Motivation

"If you think you can do a thing or think you can't do a thing, you're right." —Henry Ford

Create a Specific Vision for Change

As pointed out in Chapter 3, establishing a specific vision of your ideal destination is a vital early and ongoing step to achieving your goals. "Neuroscientists at the Massachusetts Institute of Technology have shown that when people reflect frequently on what their positive future selves will look like, they are more likely to make choices in their long-term interest rather than shortsighted ones." [1]

Positive Anticipation

Interestingly, researchers have discovered that simply looking forward to a planned activity or event, such as a vacation, can increase positive feelings. "One study discovered that people who just thought about watching their favorite movie actually raised their endorphin levels by 27 percent." [2] The anticipation of a positive planned event also has the effect of making the activity more enjoyable when it does arrive. The essence of positive anticipation is about having a positive focus and keeping our motivational spirit strong and vibrant.

Positive Thinking Insight

Self-awareness is an essential precondition for positive change; therefore, the topic to explore is what's working and what's not working in the area of desired change.

What Are Affirmations and How Can They Help You?

Affirmations are statements that reflect a positive attitude or thoughts about yourself. Affirmations can assist you with building confidence and creating strong positive beliefs about yourself.

Key Points:

Positive statements about oneself should be believable, vivid, present tense, and meaningful. Avoid "I always" and "I never" statements. Typical ways people utilize affirmations is writing them down and displaying them in key places such as on the refrigerator, lockers, bedroom nightstands, or gym bags.

Example: "I am an accurate quarterback; I am "zoned in" under pressure!"

Being Positive Allows for Engaged Focus

People who report the greatest interest in attaining money, fame, or beauty are consistently found to be less happy, and even less healthy, than those who pursue less materialistic goals.[3]

Thus, we ask ourselves what is the right kind of activity to pursue? The tool that helped psychologists answer this question is the "experience sampling method," invented by Mihalyi Csikszentmihalyi (pronounced "cheeks sent me high"); he is the Hungarian-born cofounder of positive psychology. Csikszentmihalyi's studies consisted of individuals carrying with them a pager that beeped numerous times a day. When a beep occurred, the individual pulled out a notebook and recorded what he or she was doing at that particular moment, and how much he or she was enjoying it. [3]

Csikszentmihalyi discovered what individuals really enjoy doing, not simply what they remembered having enjoyed. He found that there are 2 different types of enjoyment. One is body or physical pleasure. At mealtimes, individuals report the highest levels of well-being and happiness, on average. People especially enjoy eating in the company of others, and they disliked being interrupted by phone calls during meals or during sex. However, as human beings we are not designed to enjoy physical pleasure all day long. "The fact is, by their very nature, food and sex satiate. To continue eating or having sex beyond a certain level of satisfaction can lead to disgust."[3]

Csikszentmihalyi also discovered that there is a state many individuals value more than chocolate or sex. It is the state of *total involvement in a task*, which is challenging yet very closely matched to one's abilities and skills. This state is what people sometimes refer to as "being in the zone." [3] Csikszentmihalyi called it "flow" due to the feeling of effortless movement.

Flow often happens during physical movement; for example, skiing, running, or playing team sports. This state is assisted by music or by the action of other individuals, both of which establish a structure for our behavior (for example, being part of a musical group, dancing, or simply having a conversation with a friend).

The state of flow can also occur during solitary creative experiences; for example, drawing, painting, photography, writing, etc. The key ingredients to establishing the state of flow entails having a specific challenge that engages one hundred percent of your attention, possessing the necessary skills to meet the challenge, and receiving feedback.

"In the flow experience, elephant and rider are in perfect harmony. The elephant (automatic processes) is doing most of the work, running smoothly through the forest, while the rider (conscious thought) is completely absorbed in looking out for problems and opportunities, helping whenever he can." [3]

The Relationship between Mood, Memory, and Positive Thinking

Research has demonstrated that when people continually focus on the negative circumstances or events in their lives, they begin to feel sad.

When individuals focus on positive events, they are much happier. It is not simply a case of memory influencing mood; mood also impacts memory. In one very skillfully created experiment, psychologists James Laird and his fellow associates from Clark University studied how mood effects memory. They asked individuals to read two brief passages. The first was a sad newspaper editorial about the needless killing of dolphins during tuna fishing, and the second was a humorous story by Woody Allen.[4]

The experimenters utilized a creative method to make the participants feel happy or sad. They asked half the individuals to hold a pencil between their teeth, making sure it did not touch their lips. Without them realizing it, the lower part of their faces was smiling. The other half of the participants were asked to support just the end of the pencil with only their lips and not their teeth, without realizing it, the lower part of their face was frowning. The fact is when you force your face into a smile you actually feel happy. Likewise, when you force your face to frown you feel sad. The participants were then asked to write down everything they could recall from the two passages; the results were amazing. The individuals who had forced themselves to smile remembered lots of information from the Woody Allen story and considerably less from the story about the needless killing of dolphins. Those subjects who had been forced to frown recalled very little about the Woody Allen story and lots more from the serious editorial.[4] Their mood influenced their ability to remember the information. Similarly, when you look back on your life in a happy mood, you tend to remember life events and circumstances that worked well. And when you reflect back in an unhappy mood, you are inclined to dwell on more negative events that happened to you.

This two-way relationship between mood and memory explains why those who tend to think positively are reluctant to dwell on any misfortune in their past, which also helps them maintain a lucky life perspective!

Possessing a Positive Perspective

People that possess a positive perspective persevere and have more beneficial responses in the face of failure.

The following puzzle highlights this point: Imagine that you are in a room designed for this "test" and are given a candle, matches, and a box of pins. You are asked to attach the candle to the wall in such a manner that it can be lit and utilized as a light. Some individuals stick the pins in the wall then attempt to balance the candle on the pins, while others place their efforts in melting the bottom of the candle with a match, subsequently trying to stick the candle to the wall. Neither of these methods yields a positive result.[4]

The fact is, only a small percentage of individuals come up with the correct result; they empty the pins from the box, and then utilize two of the pins to secure the box to the wall, thus allowing for the easy placement of the candle on the pin box—puzzle solved.[4] It is without a doubt an elegant, effective, and a simple answer to this puzzle. It is also one that involves flexible thinking. The box containing the pins is not only a box; it can also be a candleholder. When the puzzle is viewed from a positive perspective, possibilities reveal themselves. One could say this is an example of having the ability to think outside the box!

Good Luck, Bad Luck Story[5]

A father and his son owned a farm. They did not have many animals, but they did own one horse. One day the horse ran away. "How terrible, what bad luck," said the neighbors.

"Good luck, bad luck, who knows?" replied the farmer. Several weeks later the horse returned, bringing with him four wild mares. "What marvelous luck," said the neighbors. "Good luck, bad luck, who knows," said the farmer. The son began to learn to ride the wild horses, but one day he was thrown and broke his leg. "What bad luck," said the neighbor. "Good luck, bad luck, who knows," replied the farmer. The next week the army came to the village to take all the young men to war. The farmer's son was still disabled with his broken leg, so he was spared. Good luck, bad luck, who knows..." [5]

The above story illustrates the value of being nonjudgmental. It avoids premature judgment of failure by reframing unwanted outcomes simply as feedback. It promotes a neutral view of negative outcomes, in addition to discouraging judgmental approaches to outcomes.

Finding the Positives in Everyday Life

Life is a constant process of adaptation, transition, and growth. The more efficient you become at finding the **positives**, focusing through obstacles, the happier, healthier, and more fulfilled your life will be. If you can perceive difficulties and setbacks as challenges to overcome and an opportunity for growth, you can change those experiences into advantages.

Finding the lessons in loss can be an effective means of putting you back in control. The reality is, every thinking, feeling, living human being experiences loss and pain at some point in their lives; no one can evade it.

When you learn to put a loss in perspective, whether it is a small loss or a big one, you are able to grow from the experience and rejoice in the good things that you enjoy and still have. The key is to find a positive reason to move on in a goal-directed fashion. For example, you can honor someone you lost by remembering the positive memories long after they are gone. Live fully and embrace your life, not just going through the motions but living in the moment. Ultimately, any type of loss provides us with lessons that can help us to live and perform more effectively in ways that we may have never imagined.

The Effect Patterns We Use to Process Information Have on Positive Thinking

The patterns that we utilize to process information are referred to as *heuristics*. They are automatic, repetitive, quite often shortcut-patterned approaches for processing information. When heuristics become reflexive and ingrained they bias our information processing by selectively establishing value to some information while ignoring other data.

Heuristics allow us to process information faster and with less effort as we progress through life; however, they also make our thinking processes prone to error and distortion if they are used in inappropriate situations. They have the potential to lure us into a mental rigidity that blinds us to the need for different thinking methods. Consequently, they often result in mental processing biases that can influence our emotional and behavioral lives in a negative manner.

9 Heuristic Examples

1) **All or Nothing Thinking:** Thinking in which events or situations are either black or white. If a situation is less than perfect, it is considered a complete failure. (For example, saying, "My free throws are off...I see now how I am going to play during this game," after only one missed attempt.)

2) **Overgeneralizations**: This occurs when we tend to view one temporary quality or event as an overall permanent state of affairs. Quite often we find ourselves utilizing the words, "always" or "never" to describe an event or situation. (For example, "I never get fair calls with the refs; they never call fouls in my favor!")

3) **Jumping to Conclusions:** Arbitrarily interpreting situations without facts to support one's conclusions. It includes mind reading ("I don't think she likes me at all!") and fortune telling ("I know I am going to mess this up...no doubt about it.").

4) **Magnification:** Exaggerating the importance of one problem and shortcoming. ("If I don't make this play, my teammates will hate me...for sure!")

5) **Minimization:** Entails minimizing your desirable qualities and skills. ("I am not really that good, it was a very lucky 3-point shot.")

Also, minimizing risks and losses to manage fear and personal conflicts are characteristic of minimization. (For example, "I didn't want to beat him anyway because this is just a local tournament… not a big deal.")

6) **Emotional Reasoning**: This happens when we assume that the way we feel is the way things really are. ("I feel mediocre; I must be a second-rate basketball player.")

7) **Labeling:** This involves the use of irrational name-calling against yourself and/or others. (For example, "I am such a loser!" after only making one error.)

8) **Personalization**: Viewing situations only in terms of yourself and holding yourself responsible for occurrences that are not 100% under your control. (Coach Johnson did not say hello when she walked by; I must have offended her!)

9) **Confirmation bias**: This occurs when we accept only information that supports our current beliefs while rejecting or finding fault with any data that does not support our current beliefs.

Heuristic Story

"A man was rowing his boat upstream on a very misty morning. Suddenly, he saw another boat coming downstream, not trying to avoid him. It was coming straight at him. He shouted, "Be careful! Be careful!" but the boat came right at him, and his boat was almost sunk. The man became very angry and began to shout at the other person to give him a piece of his mind. But when he looked closely, he saw that there was no one in the other boat. It turned out that the boat just got loose and went downstream. All his anger vanished, and he laughed and laughed. If our perceptions are not correct, they may give us a lot of bad feelings."[6] – Thich Nhat Hanh

Self-Fulfilling Prophecies

The expectation of something going wrong is referred to as a *self-fulfilling prophecy;* this means that the *expectation* of something going wrong actually assists in causing it to occur. This phenomenon is common in both exercise and competitive sport environments. Negative self-fulfilling prophecies are simply psychological barriers that ultimately lead to a vicious cycle. When you have an expectation of failure, this leads to actual failure, which decreases confidence and increases expectations of some sort of future failure. For example, a baseball player in a slump starts to expect to strike out, which facilitates increased anxiety, thus decreasing concentration, which in turn typically results in lowered expectations and poorer performances. The story of Roger Bannister illuminates how someone can overcome an established self-fulfilling prophecy. He broke the 4-minute mile. Prior to 1954, the majority of people believed that it was impossible to run a mile in less than 4 minutes. However, there were runners that came very close to breaking the 4-minute mile; runners were timed at 4:03 and 4:01. The collective belief remained that to beat the 4-minute mile was physiologically impossible. Roger Bannister believed that it was possible to beat the 4-minute mile barrier under the right conditions, and that is exactly what he did! [7]

Roger's goal accomplishment and self-belief was very impressive; however, what's really thought-provoking is that in the next few years, approximately a dozen runners beat the 4-minute mile! [7] We may ask ourselves, why did this occur? Did everyone begin to train harder after witnessing what Roger had accomplished, and subsequently become faster? The answer is no. What occurred was that the runners viewed the situation from a positive perspective after Roger had broken the 4-minute mile.

The fact is, prior to Roger Bannister breaking this collective negative self-fulfilling prophecy, runners had been putting psychological limits on their perceived abilities and related skills. Such psychological barriers serve to decrease motivation and limit goal achievement and overall success. However, here we have Roger Bannister "opening our eyes" to the power of positive thinking; it is truly inspiring!

Remember:

The greatest barriers in our pursuit of excellence are *psychological barriers* that we impose on ourselves, often without realizing it. As our beliefs about limits change, limits themselves change.[8] The story of Roger Bannister highlights this profound point very well.

Paul Grayson's Positive Thinking

England and Northampton rugby player Paul Grayson typically had the responsibility for place-kicking. Paul scored the most points in both the 1997 and 1998 Five Nations championships for England. Paul explained his mental approach to successful goal-kicking.

"There are occasions when winning the points in the match are down to me. When I am facing the posts for a conversion of a penalty, I don't think about missing. It doesn't enter my head. I am there to score the goal and make the points....

My mental focus comes from **self-belief.** The knowledge that I can do what I have to do. As soon as you let doubt creep in, you may as well give up. You have to set yourself goals and then analyze your mental approach as well as your physical approach." [9]

The Power of Self-Belief

In 1952, a young British doctor, Dr. Albert Mason, made a mistake; it was an error that brought him short-lived scientific glory. He attempted to treat a fifteen-year-old boy's warts utilizing hypnosis. Mason and other clinicians had successfully performed hypnosis to get rid of the warts; however, this was a particularly challenging case. The boy's skin looked like an elephant hide, except for his chest area; this area was unaffected.[10]

Mason's initial hypnosis session focused on one arm. While the boy was in a hypnotic trance, he was told that the skin on that arm would heal and turn into healthy, normal-looking skin. Upon the boy returning a week later, Mason was very pleased to see that the arm looked healthy. However, when the boy went to the referred specialist who had previously unsuccessfully attempted to help him with skin grafts, Mason learned that he had made a medical mistake. The specialist's eyes were wide with amazement when he saw the boy's arm. It was at this time that Mason was informed that the boy was actually suffering from a disease called genetic ichthyosis. The young British doctor and the boy had accomplished something that until that time was considered impossible. The hypnosis sessions continued with stunning results. The majority of the boy's skin came to look like the healthy arm that had been successfully treated at the initial hypnosis session. The boy, who had been cruelly teased in school because of his disformed-looking skin, went on to have a normal life. This story is a great example of the power positive thinking in action.[10]

Controlling Moods

When you are able to control your mood, you are able to focus on the positives and not upset yourself needlessly over things that don't actually matter, unfamiliar situations, or things that you simply cannot control. Importantly noted, mood control is dependent on focus control. The great news is that it's within your reach. Controlling your mood is basically a matter of looking for the good in yourself, in your situation, in the world, as well as seeking out the opportunities that exist within obstacles.

Uncontrolled negative emotions inhibit awareness and growth and weaken your motivational spirit. The sooner you learn to shift away from negative thinking to positive thinking, the sooner you will be able to take control of your performance as well as your life. The key is to gain control over your negative emotions by taking control of your *focus* and *thoughts*. If you find yourself in a negative focus pattern, consider the following strategies.

4 Tips to Assist in Controlling Moods

1) Try to get more sleep. Negative thinking is more likely to happen when you are fatigued or tired; thus, finding a way to get enough sleep is a daily goal for everyone reading this book!

2) Find ways to decrease stress in your life. Persistent stress in your life makes you more susceptible to negative shifts in mood.

3) Stay open to the positive emotions and energy of those around you because they can provide you with much-needed positive energy, perspective, as well as motivation.

4) At least once a day, ask yourself, "Where is my focus, my full attention? Is it on the positives or the negatives?"

The Impact of Music on Mood Control

Music influences physiology and mood. Research findings highlight that music can facilitate exercise performance by decreasing the feeling of fatigue, increasing the levels of mental excitement, limiting some of the painful physical sensations experienced with exercise, as well as improving motor coordination. In a study conducted at Pavia University in Pavia, Italy, researchers found that music has a constant dynamic influence on cardio-respiratory responses. Music crescendos (loudness or intensity) increase systolic/diastolic blood pressures and heart rate, while decrescendos and silent pauses create a reduction in heart rate and other variables.[11]

The Power of Positive Emotions

Positive psychology author Barbara Fredrickson has discovered some interesting information regarding the power of emotions. She found that "there is a ratio of positive emotions to negative emotions for your brain to function at its best; this ratio is 75/25."[1] Additionally, we should be aware of another ratio, according to Marcial Losada; this number is 2.9013. Yes, initially this seems like a random number, however after a decade of research on performance teams, its significance was revealed. "Based on Losada's extensive mathematical modeling, 2.9013 is the ratio of positive to negative interactions necessary to make a corporate team successful. This means that it takes about 3 positive comments, experiences, or expressions to fend off the languishing effects of just 1 negative." [2]

This is not some mysterious mathematical formula. Losada observed many examples of it in action. For example, he once worked with a global mining company suffering from process losses greater than 10 percent; unsurprisingly, he found that their positivity ratio was only 1.15. But after team leaders were instructed to give more positive feedback and encourage more positive interactions, their teams' average ratio increased to 3.56. And in turn, they made giant strides in production, improving their performance by over 40 percent." [2]

Knowing the impact of being positive, imagine then the power you have to influence the performance of not just yourself but others around you! When your brain constantly scans for and focuses on the positives in everyday life, you benefit from two key tools available to you: *gratitude* and *happiness*.

According to Psychologist Robert Emmons, who has spent the majority of his career studying gratitude, "Few things in life are as integral to our well-being. Countless studies have shown that consistently grateful people are more energetic, emotionally intelligent, forgiving, and less likely to be depressed, anxious, or lonely." [2] Importantly noted here, it's not that we are grateful because we are happier; actually, gratitude has shown to be an important *cause* of positive results and happiness.

"Studies have shown that optimists set more goals (and more difficult goals) than pessimists, put more effort into attaining those goals, stay more engaged in the face of difficulty, in addition to rising above obstacles more easily. Optimists also cope better in high stress situations and are better able to maintain high levels of well-being during times of hardship, all skills that are crucial to high performance in a demanding work environment." [2] This piece of research highlights that optimism is a very powerful predictor of effective performance.

Plan for Positive Action

There are two ways in which you can develop positive change. *First*, you can change your focus. *Second*, you can change your environment. If you change only your environment while maintaining the same focus, odds greatly favor nothing changing. However, if you change your perspective (positive thinking) and focus (goal directed), positive change is guaranteed!

Meditation

Neuroscientists have discovered an interesting phenomenon that happens to monks who spend years meditating; they strengthen their left prefrontal cortex, the region of the brain most responsible for feeling happy. Importantly noted here, you do not have to spend years meditating as a monk if you do not wish. You have another option of taking just 5 minutes daily to watch your breath go in and out, trying to remain calm and patient while doing so. If you find your mind wandering from the task at hand, slowly bring back your focus by concentrating, once again, on your breathing. The fact is, quality meditation takes practice, but it is a powerful tool to facilitate a feeling of calm and happiness. Studies have demonstrated that minutes immediately after meditating, people experience a feeling of calmness, as well as increased awareness and empathy; this has the effect of "opening the door" to positive thinking. Research has also highlighted the fact that consistent meditation can permanently rewire the brain in such a way as to lower stress and improve immune function.[2]

Living in the Here and Now

We must live in the present time because *only* the present is real; *only* in the present moment can we be fully alive. As human beings, we tend to postpone being alive to the future, sometimes the distant future; we don't actually know when. In the present moment is the time to be alive; otherwise, we might never be alive at all in our entire life. Thus, a priority *daily goal* is to be in the present moment, to be aware that you are here, in the present moment, and the *only* time to be alive is the present moment.

Words of Wisdom

A smile has the potential to relax as many as hundreds of muscles in your face, as well as relax your nervous system!

Teachers such as Buddha and Jesus have told the same story for millennia. Our genes do not determine the quality of our lives; beliefs are what control our happiness and well-being. The fact is, positive thoughts are a biological requirement for a happy, healthy life. In the insightful words of Gandhi:

> *"Your beliefs become your thoughts*
> *Your thoughts become your words*
> *Your words become your actions*
> *Your actions become your habits*
> *Your habits become your values*
> *Your values become your destiny"* [10]

Plan a Positive Path and Follow It

You have the power to decide to remain positive. Staying positive will without a doubt lead to higher quality training, better performances, and a happier life path.

4 Steps to Establishing a Positive Life Path:

First, *create a vision* of a better way of perceiving and responding to experiences, situations, and encounters with others. Second, establish a clearly defined plan with realistic goals. Third, make a confident decision to act on the plan, again and again, until a routine of positive change is established. Fourth, always avoid spending your energy on things beyond your control.

Closing Thought

When you are effective at eliminating the barrier of "im" from impossible and focus on possibilities, goal attainment becomes much more likely for you. Subsequently, belief and the ability to focus give rise to new and exciting realties and possibilities!

Chapter 10

Imagery: *A Vital Tool for Envisioning Ourselves Accomplishing our Goals*

"We taped a lot of famous pictures on the locker room door, all holding the Stanley Cup. We'd stand back and look at them and envision ourselves doing it. I really believe if you visualize yourself doing something, you can make that image come true...I must have rehearsed it ten thousand times. And when it came true it was like an electric jolt went up my spine." [1]

—Wayne Gretzky

In your everyday life, as well as your athletic performance life, do your thoughts and images assist you in creating the life that you would like to live? You can utilize your positive thoughts, images, and experiences to guide your performances and your life in constructive ways. Mental imagery provides an opportunity to create a better reality and allows you to deal successfully with challenges, problems, or events in your mind prior to confronting them in real life. If a challenge that you have prepared for mentally does arise, you are in a better position to cope with it or focus through it.

Imagery

Imagery is essentially creating or recreating an experience in our minds utilizing all of our senses. Imagery is often referred to as visualization; however, visualization suggests *just* seeing the image, while the definition of imagery includes using all of the senses, making it polysensory, not just simply a visual experience. Imagery allows us to experience the task, and if we can see ourselves performing the task, subsequently we are much more likely to believe that it can actually happen.

Why Imagery Works

Imagery is often referred to as a mental process. While this is true, it is also a physical process. Many processes, such as feelings, thoughts, and imaginal experiences, involve the brain, nervous system, and body; therefore, technically speaking, imagery is both a mental process as well as a physical one.

Research has shown that mental practice is not purely mental because it activates the same neurocognitive templates/pathways in the brain that are utilized for athletic performance. The concept of functional equivalence suggests that the same neural networks used in visual processing are also used in visual imagery; this theory finds that these templates are responsible for initiating and sustaining motor activity. Every time a skill is performed, mentally or physically, either the cognitive template or the physical template becomes stronger, thus increasing the likelihood of successfully performing the skill in the future.[1] In light of this information, mental practice is a strong choice to supplement any well-designed goal plan.

Imagery practice, sometimes referred to as imagery rehearsal, should involve the use of all of the senses (also known as imagery modalities). The goal for optimal use of this motivational ingredient entails using sight, touch, taste, sound, and smell when practicing imagery.

The 5 Characteristics of Successful Imagery Practice[1]

1) **Real-Time**: The image should be as much like real life as possible, and this includes the timing. For example, if a sprinter's time is 40 seconds on the track, his imagery should happen as close to 40

seconds as possible. There are times where an athlete might benefit from slowing a skill down. For example, if he or she is trying to examine their form, or having difficulty controlling the image, in most instances, imagery should happen in real-time.

2) **Vivid**: Imagery is more effective if it is especially vivid. The difference between HD televisions and televisions from 15 years ago is a great example of this point. In an HD TV, the picture is very clear and much like reality. It can take a considerable amount of time to develop vivid imagery, but extremely vivid imagery is most likely related to the utilization of multiple or all our senses; therefore, it is best to attempt to include all senses when using imagery.

3) **Positive**: The goal is to experience what you want to happen, not want you want to avoid when imaging. The idea is to stay away from imagining negative performance outcomes. However, there may be a few instances in which imagining a negative outcome is beneficial. For example, a quarterback wants to imagine how to be prepared and quickly react in the event that he misses a snap. This will allow this athlete to be better prepared in the actual situation.

4) **Controllability**: Controllability relates to the control that we have over the happenings of an imaginal experience. The question to ask is, "Does the image do what I want it to do?" Often times, upon being introduced to imagery practice, individuals do not have a lot of control over their images. For example, a soccer player might be able to kick the ball but is unable get it into the goal.

5) **Consistency**: Similar to all motivational ingredients discussed in this book, imagery should be used on a consistent basis to be most effective. You can spend as little as 5 minutes a day, 5 days a week to maintain consistent imagery practice. However, if practiced 7 days per week, reaping the benefits from consistent imagery practice will only increase, as positive daily habits lead to positive outcomes.

Research Highlights the Benefits of Consistent Imagery Practice

Research has highlighted that imagery rehearsal is vital for winning the mind game in sports. Nearly all athletes and coaches utilize imagery to help them train and compete. In a survey carried out by Doug Jowdy and Shirley Durtschi, it was discovered that 90% of the athletes and 94% of the coaches asked at the Olympic Training Center in Colorado Springs utilized imagery in their sport; 20% of the athletes used imagery every day. When asked why they used imagery, 80% of the athletes stated that they used it to prepare for competition, 48% utilized it to deal with errors in technique, 44% used it to learn new skills, and 40% used imagery for relaxation. When asked about the effectiveness, 97% of the athletes and 100% of the coaches agreed that imagery does enhance performance. Imagery is nearly universally viewed as an effective means to improve athletic performance.[2]

The Correlation between Imagery and Goal Setting

Imagery helps athletes select goals and also helps fuel motivation to achieve them. This motivational function of imagery was described in a 1998 paper by Shelly Taylor and her colleagues from the University of California on the utilization of imagination as a method of self-regulating: "The term imagination may be used quite specifically to refer to the mental activities that people engage in when they want to get from a current point in time and place to a subsequent one, having accomplished something in between, such as going on a trip or writing a paper. An activity fundamental to this task is mental simulation. Mental simulation is the imitative representation of some event or series of events." [2]

Imagery is closely related to goal setting because it assists in the choice of both direction and intensity of effort; it assists in fueling motivation. Repeated imagery of a desired result helps bridge the gap between a far-off goal outcome and present-day reality, seeming to bring the desired goal closer and motivating you to work hard in order to achieve it.

Imagery Perspectives[1]

The ways imagery can be utilized to benefit performance and skill development are limited only by your imagination! There are 5 perspectives you might use to create or recreate goal-directed experiences.

1) The **visual-internal** form of imagery entails viewing what is going on as though you were actually there performing; it is also known as associative imagery. A downhill skier, for example, using this form of first-person perspective would visualize each bump and turn approaching in his imagined run down the mountain and would see the scenery flashing by as if his eyes were a video camera.

2) In contrast to visual-internal, **visual-external** imagery is similar to watching yourself through a camera; it is also known as dissociative imagery; it is a third-person visualization in which you step outside your own body momentarily to watch yourself perform. Here the downhill skier would picture himself hurtling down the mountain crouched in the tuck position, carving turns or jumping as though seeing himself on a television sport show. This is the most common imagery perspective utilized by athletes.

3) The **kinesthetic form** of imagery entails recreating the physical feeling of performance. The downhill skier would imagine the feeling of pushing his heels back and shins forward in the ski boot, noticing the sensation in the knees as he bumps, and the thigh muscles begin to burn toward the end of a very long run.

4) **Visual-internal kinesthetic** is a combination of visual-internal and kinesthetic imagery. It entails experiencing a performance through your own eyes while at the same time recreating the bodily feelings.

5) **Visual-external kinesthetic** combines visual-external with kinesthetic imagery. You visualize your performance from the outside while at the same time recreating the physical sensations.

10 Ways Consistent Imagery Practice Will Benefit You

1) **Learning new skills/enhancing physical skills**: Imagery practice used in this way is often called imaginal practice, mental practice, and symbolic rehearsal.

2) **Developing plans and strategies**: Researchers have demonstrated that imagery is helpful for devising strategies and developing plans in sports such as canoeing, football, and wrestling. Using imagery for planning permits you to try many approaches to the same problem until finding the one that suits you.

3) **Building confidence**: Imagining skillful execution of performing a physical act greatly enhances confidence by providing a vicarious experience of a performance accomplishment. Additionally, athletes can utilize imagery as a performance boost immediately before competition, like a diver who envisions a perfect dive while standing on the springboard, or over a period of time as they build a better self-image. Another example, a backup quarterback who utilizes imagery to practice what he would do if he had to step into the game and take over the team leadership role.

4) **Enhancing motivation**: Repeating imagery of desired results can help make your distant goals seem more attainable, thus motivating you to achieve them.

5) **Psyching up**: Imagery practice used for energizing an athlete just before a competition should evoke images of physiological arousal.

6) **Energy management**: Reducing anxiety; imagining a calm, peaceful experience; and embracing the physiological sensations associated with it can bring about a calming effect.

7) **Stress management**: Imagery can be a very useful way to prepare for stressful sport situations. An athlete entering his or her first Olympic Games, for example, may never have experienced an actual Olympic competition; however, through imagery he or she can visualize attending the opening ceremonies and competing in the event. The athlete imagines how they would feel in such a situation; if he or she feels anxious and stressed by the imagery,

the real-life experience is quite likely to be similarly stressful. Imagery gives the athlete the opportunity to mentally prepare effective coping strategies, such as deep breathing, positive self-dialogue, muscle relaxation, in addition to changing their focus of concentration. Preparing to handle stressful situations in this manner allows him or her to approach the situation with greater confidence, while feeling less stress during the event.

8) **Rehabbing from injury**: Injured athletes can utilize imagery to maintain attention, skills, and motivation during the rehabilitation process. For example, Kevin, a basketball player with an ACL injury who is unable to play for eight to nine months, can mentally practice his basketball skills such as free throws, passing, and defending on a regular if not daily basis. In addition to strengthening cognitive skill templates, imagery serves to increase the motivation of injured athletes, such as Kevin. Increased motivation benefits the athlete if it leads to greater adherence to and effort put forth in the rehabilitation program.

9) **Sharpening focus**: Positive performance imagery strengthens your mental focus and confidence because it centers you on the feeling and concentration of your best performances. However, even the best performers usually did not have good control over their mental imagery when they *first* began utilizing it. They perfected this skill through determined daily use and focused practice.

10) **Mental imagery for coping skills**: The mental practice of your preferred response makes it possible to enter a potentially threatening situation feeling better prepared, less fearful, more in control and confident; it gives you something positive to focus on in order to get back on track quickly when you actually face a challenging, sometimes unexpected situation.

Remember:

A key reason that mental imagery can be so valuable in a performance context is that the human brain cannot differentiate between an imagined experience and a real experience; both are equally real in your brain. The same regions of the brain light up in an imagined experience or imagined performance as a real experience or performance.[3] For that reason, positive performance imagery has a lot of potential. When you repeatedly imagine yourself doing what you want to become, you are placing yourself on a path to create a more positive future reality. The successful completion of repeating skills, performance moves, or experiences in your mind is often as good as doing them in your physical reality because you can potentially do them perfectly and your brain understands them as real.

Developing Imagery Skills

No matter how good or how limited your mental imagery skills are today, you can improve them by practicing daily, both at home and on-site in your training or performance environment. The more quality mental imagery you execute, the more quickly your imagery will improve. If you have never done any systematic imagery training, begin with simple, familiar images or skills. For the next week or two set aside five minutes a day, either before going to practice or before going to sleep, to work on your imagery skills. Let yourself relax while shutting your eyes. As a rule, you should get into a pattern of doing approximately 15 minutes of quality imagery every day, make it a positive routine. Besides helping you improve your physical and technical skills, mental imagery is itself a great focusing exercise. This point cannot be overemphasized.

In many instances, mental imagery is the first step that performers take to improve certain skills or overcome expected problems; imagery gets you started. It is not time-consuming, and you can do it yourself wherever and whenever you so choose. Sometimes mental imagery can itself lead to your overcoming a specific problem or improving your performance. *Remember*, the typical sequence is to start with mental imagery of what you want to happen, practice the imagined skill or coping tactic in a real-life training situation, introduce the skill or focusing approach in a simulated competition situation, and finally utilize it in the real performance event.

An Example of Imagery at Its Best: Sylvie Bernie

"I did my dives in my head all the time. At night, before going to sleep, I always did my dives. Ten dives. I started with a front dive, the first one that I had to do at the Olympics, and I did everything as if I was actually there. I saw myself in the pool at the Olympics doing my dives. If the dive was wrong, I went back and started over. For me, it was better than a workout. I felt like I was on the board. Sometimes I would take the weekend off and do imagery five times a day. It took me a long time to control my images and perfect my imagery, maybe a year, doing it every day. At first, I couldn't see myself. I always saw everyone else, or I would see my dives wrong all the time. I would get an image of hurting myself or tripping on the board, or I would see something done really badly. As I continued to work at it, I got to the point where I could feel myself on the board doing a perfect dive and hear the crowd yelling at the Olympics. I worked at it so much, it got to the point that I could do all the dives easily. Sometimes I would even be in the middle of a conversation with someone, and I would think of one of my dives and do it (in my mind)." [3]

4 Strategies for Helping You Improve Your Imagery Skills

1) Break the skill/performance down. For example, if Molly, an ice skater, cannot experience her whole routine, she needs to select a small part and add sections as her skills improve.

2) Perform the skill and then imagine the skill. Athletes often benefit from doing imagery immediately following the execution of the actual skill. For example, Tyler, a pitcher who struggles with doing imagery of his fast ball, should close his eyes right after the pitch and try to recreate the optimal pitch that he is seeking.

3) Practice imagery of everyday items. Practice imagery of something that you are very familiar with, for example, a room in your house, or a familiar location, etc.
4) Watch other athletes and performers execute the desired skill; it assists in keeping the image present.

Examples of the Five Senses Utilized through Imagery

1) **Sounds**: The sound of a plate as it hits the ground and smashes, the sound of a tennis ball as it contacts the sweet spot of a tennis racket.
2) **Feeling**: The slippery smoothness of wet a bar of soap.
3) **Smells**: The scent of freshly ground coffee, the fragrance of your favorite perfume or aftershave, the strong smell of chlorine as you enter an indoor swimming pool, the smell of recently mown grass on a hot summer's day.
4) **Tastes**: The bitterness of dark chocolate, the taste of pepper on the tip of your tongue, the sweetness of honey.
5) **Sights**: A long, sandy beach that stretches to a point where it unites with the horizon; all colors of the rainbow, consecutively: red, orange, yellow, green, blue, indigo, violet; your favorite video game; riding a bicycle on a rough, mountainous path.

Questions to Think About

Try to recognize which senses are really vivid and which are difficult to induce. Can you see movement in your images? Are you able to imagine in color? Make brief notes in response to these questions and write down anything else that seems significant about your images. This will be very useful information in subsequent imagery experiences. Now try utilizing all five senses to create images. Begin with something very simple like making and then eating your favorite sandwich, or try the following exercise:

The Orange Imagery Scripted Exercise

An exercise that can also help you to assess your imagery ability is the orange imagery exercise:

Sit comfortably in your chair with your feet placed on the ground. Once you are comfortable, close your eyes. If you are not comfortable closing your eyes, pick one point to fix your attention upon. Take a few deep breaths....see yourself standing in your kitchen...look at the color of the walls....feel the temperature in the room....as you look around the room, you notice several oranges sitting on the counter.... walk over to them....look at the color of the oranges....see the bright orange....pick up one orange from the counter....feel the weight of the orange in your hand ...bring the orange up to your nose and smell the peel...set the orange down onto a cutting board....you notice a knife next to the cutting board...pick it up by the handle....look at the shine of the blade...feel the solid handle....when you are ready, carefully slice into the orange...hear the knife cut through the peel and into the flesh of the orange...set the knife down and bring half of the orange to your nose....smell the scent of the orange ...then bring the orange to your mouth and take a bite...(pause)...when you are ready, take several deep breaths, and open your eyes.

This scripted imagery example provides cues to all of the senses: **sight** (seeing the color), **sound** (hearing the knife cut the orange), **touch** (feeling the weight), **smell** (of the peel), **taste** (biting into it). You can create such imagery scripts that are applicable to your goals. In the process, you will discover the power of imagery!

What Is Peak Performance Imagery?

Some characteristics of a peak performance include being very confident, possessing a positive attitude about performance, a feeling of being in total control, and complete involvement in the task at hand; the performance is exceptional, seemingly surpassing typical levels of play.

Please think and reflect upon this definition. In your experience, how many peak performances have you had? Peak performances do not occur often, but this is often what we seek, an excellent performance. Peak performance imagery involves using *all* of your senses. The goal is to get a snapshot of the power of the mind, as well as how imagery is very beneficial to you.

Recall, Rate, and Reflect Exercise

Recall a memory of a peak performance that you have experienced in your sport, occupation, or in everyday life. Describe your thoughts, vision, feelings, sensations, and emotional responses by writing them down.

Your goal here is to use all of your senses (seeing, hearing, tasting, smelling, and feeling). Make a taped recording of yourself reading your peak experience, after you have written it down. Then, rate the experience using the following imagery checklist:

Rate Peak Performance

Rating Scale	Low		Medium		High
Overall vividness	1	2	3	4	5
Real-time	1	2	3	4	5
Feeling	1	2	3	4	5
Hearing	1	2	3	4	5
Control	1	2	3	4	5
Tasting	1	2	3	4	5
Smelling	1	2	3	4	5
Seeing	1	2	3	4	5

Self-Reflection Activity

Place a check mark next to the following areas that you would like to improve using imagery practice:

Building Confidence _____

Maintaining Focus _____

Learning a New Skill _____

Energy Management _____

Psyching Up _____

Relaxing _____

Creating and Developing New Strategies _____

Managing Pain _____

Rehabilitating from a Sports Injury _____

Skill Correction after Errors Occur in Performance Execution _____

Reinforcing Peak Performance Moments _____

3 Ways to Hold onto Your Peak Performance Using Imagery

1) After a successful performance, analyze it utilizing each of your five senses: what you saw, heard, smelled, tasted, or felt at the time of the peak performance.
2) Take particular note of any self-dialogue that was taking place inside your head and the influence it had on your performance; possibly there was no self-dialogue whatsoever.
3) Practice recreating the *key indicators* of success in your mental warm-ups and mental practices.

Post-Performance Review

Even the most disappointing effort can be changed into a valuable experience if something positive can be abstracted from it. The practice of imagery to create a replay of your performance is often one of the simplest and most effective methods to analyze it. Conducting your own detailed replays of poor performance might provide the clue to technical faults about which you would otherwise remain unaware. Using imagery in this manner will also help you to recognize *patterns of behavior* or methods of preparation that contribute to good or bad performances.

Imagery Review Facilitation

To facilitate a review, plan to start the session in the same way you would for imagery practice, but while imagining yourself performing, slow the movement down and proceed to go through a *mental checklist* of all the vital technical aspects of the skill in question. When analyzing performance during imagery, it is a great idea to capture the key elements of technique with labels that act as vivid reference points during ensuing performances. For example, just before take-off, long jumpers prepare to transfer forward momentum into upward momentum by lowering their center of gravity and then producing an upward surge of the leading leg. They often capture the essence of this two-part maneuver with the labels *sink* and *drive*, which precisely sum up the required process!

Increasing your awareness of the critical aspects of technique in this fashion improves your chances of accurately identifying performance errors. Use a notepad immediately following a successful performance to write down everything you learned, or instead use a recording device, perhaps your phone. If you are injured or currently experiencing below-par form, attempt to complete the exercise retrospectively, with reference to your last peak performance.

Case Study Example: Susan

Susan is a 17-year old gymnast: she is talented and has a goal of earning a gymnastics scholarship for college. Recently, she has been feeling like she is "stuck" and not prepared to go on to the next level of competitive gymnastics. New moves and techniques on the balance beam are scary for her; she has never experienced real fear of injury before, and she wonders if this is what happens to "old people" like her neighbors, Joe and Carol Murphy. Susan states, "I'm feeling tired, but I know I must put in the time to master these new performance moves, or I'll never be able to perform them as well as I should," She has been getting shin splints from the extended workouts, and the intense pain is starting to interfere with her floor routine.

Susan has a big regional meet coming up, which she has been to but never competed in before. She is excited but also nervous about it, afraid that the enormous university gym that it is held in will just make her even more nervous.

She is attempting to complete four classes with an A average, and her biology class requires extra lab class time, two days per week. Susan is also managing lots of stress at home, and she is worried about having to do lots of extra "homework" that I might give her. She asks: "Can we do it all in two hours? Because that's all I really have time for with my current schedule."

Assessing Susan's Situation

Susan should utilize imagery because she is having difficulty reaching that "next level." She is experiencing fatigue, suffering the effects of over-training, feeling fearful of a new environment in which she has never competed, in addition to anticipating and needing to prepare for an upcoming regional meet. The use of imagery helps athletes such as Susan to learn and enhance physical skills, strategize, mentally prepare for competition, correct mistakes, plan ahead, relax, and build confidence, all of which Susan has cited as being concerns.

I point out to Susan that research has shown that mental practice is not purely mental because it also activates the same neuro-cognitive templates/pathways in the brain that are utilized for her athletic performance. Every time a performance task is executed, physically or mentally, neuro-cognitive pathways in the brain become stronger by the use of imagery practice, thereby increasing the probability of effectively performing the desired skill. [1]

Upon providing Susan with this foundational information, I introduce her to the orange imagery scripted exercise as a basic introduction. She can use imagery before and after performing a task, during training, at home, aproximately fifteen minutes a day, ideally at least five days a week. Susan's imagery goals rest upon creating a *systematic plan* that includes both in and out of practice, focusing on what she *wants* to happen and not on what she wants to avoid.

Resembling all motivational ingredients, imagery skill is acquired through *consistent* practice. Some individuals are good at it, whereas others may have difficulty being able to get an image in their minds. Ultimately, there are two essential ingredients needed to acquire quality images: **1**) *controllability* and **2**) *vividness*. Quality images utilize all of the senses to make images as vivid as possible. It is essential for Susan to create as closely as possible the actual experience in her mind, paying close attention to environmental details, such as the type of surface layout of the facility, in addition to closeness of the spectators.

Susan's degree of successful mental imaging is based upon her ability to manipulate her images in a manner that allows her to control the image. Controlling the image will allow Susan to picture what she wants to happen instead of making errors. I am inclined to say that *controlling* one's image is quite possibly the most significant aspect of successful imagery. I am of this opinion because if you cannot manipulate and control your image, you will not be able to get the image to serve its intended purpose. Sport psychology research shows that athletes develop and refine their performance by utilizing imagery that is both controllable and vivid. [4]

Closing Thoughts

Imagery is an amazing psychological tool, which remains a preeminent means for enhancing performance, reviewing skills, solving problems, facilitating recovery from injury, focusing attention, building confidence, and managing stress.

Imagery is a very complex and rich phenomenon, making it advantageous to utilize for the competing athlete, as well as someone simply seeking to reach their desired goals—this means all of us! It is a proven method to pre-create and establish successful blueprints for desired performance. Imagery is an invaluable motivational ingredient for you to use in pursuit of reaching your goals and realizing your dreams!

Chapter 11

Time:
The Most Important Reason to Stay Connected to Your Motivational Spirit

Positive Anticipation:

With each passing week ...with each passing day...with each passing hour there is less time for setting goals that entail positive anticipation. Highlighted in Chapter 9, researchers have discovered that simply looking forward to a planned activity or event, such as a vacation, can increase positive feelings; this essence of positive anticipation is about positive focus and keeping our motivational spirit solid as a rock!

With each passing week... With each passing day... With each passing hour...

I can attest to the power of positive anticipation as it pertains to looking forward to vacations and the long-lasting effects of those experiences. During the years 2002-04, my wife and I lived in San Jose, California. At this time, I was pursuing a BA in Psychology from John F. Kennedy University. During my breaks from classes, we would plan awesome trips that involved lots of beauty! Obviously, this is been quite some time ago. At this point, however, the feelings that are elicited when I view the following pictures connects me with those experiences and brings about positive feelings; this is representative of our emotional memory. Positive anticipation quite often leads to memorable experiences, and this is our ultimate goal in life as human beings…to look back at the end and reflect on our many memorable and meaningful experiences that add depth and meaning to who we are and life itself.

Outdoor Beauty, Fun, and Memorable Experiences:
In September 2003, my wife and I discovered some of the beauty that California has to offer.

Yosemite Falls, CA

Yosemite Falls, CA

The Tunnel Tree, Yosemite, CA

Putting it all in perspective…

Burnie Falls, CA

Lassen Peak & Manzanita Lake, CA

Mt. Shasta, CA (The view from our KOA cabin!)

We watched the sunset in Trinidad, CA. We hiked up the bluffs for this amazing view.

Mill Creek Resort, CA. The deck where we ate breakfast. The resort was quaint and rustic. There was a rambling creek behind our cabin (loved it!), and their breakfast food was great! You may be wondering, how I remember the breakfast was great after such a long period of time? The fact is, during this period, 2002-04, my wife was very much into the hobby of scrapbooking; she captured these experiences with creativity and writing down what happened. This is a testament to keeping a record of events and goals, as I speak of in this book.

We watched hummingbirds each morning at Mill Creek Resort, CA.

"The Humming-Bird," by Jones Very

Like thoughts that flit across the mind,
Leaving no lasting trace behind,
The humming-bird darts to and fro,
Comes, vanishes before we know.
While thoughts may be but airy things
That come and go on viewless wings,
Nor form nor substance e'en possess,
Nor number know, or more or less,
This leaves an image, well defined,
To be a picture of the mind;
Its tiny form and colors bright
In memory live, when lost to sight.
There oft it comes at evening's hour,
To flutter still from flower to flower;
Then vanish midst the gathering shade,
Its momentary visit paid.

Golden Gate Bridge, CA. (Me, January 2004) *I never walked or rode a bike across this bridge while living in CA. Thus, I have a goal of returning to do just that! Here, we have another example of the power of positive anticipation…a goal is created that puts a smile on my face!

NOTES

Introduction:

1) Rock, David. *Your Brain at Work: Strategies for Overcoming Distraction, Regaining Focus and Working Smarter All Day Long.* New York: Harper Collins, 2010.

Chapter 1:

1) Murphy, Shane M. *The Sport Psych Handbook: A Complete Guide to Today's Best Mental Training Techniques.* Champaign, IL: Human Kinetics, 2005. P. 3

2) Karageorghis, Costas I., and Peter C. Terry. *Inside Sport Psychology.* Champaign, IL: Human Kinetics, 2011. P.60, 62

3) Noyd, Robert K., Jerome A. Krueger, and Kendra M. Hill. *Biology: Organisms and Adaptations.* Boston, MA: Cengage Learning, 2014.

4) Nurmi, J.-E (1992). "Age differences in adult life goals, concerns, and their temporal extension: A life course approach to future-oriented motivation." *Journal of Behavioral Development,* 15, 478-508.

5) Cross, S., Markus, H. (1991). "Possible selves across the life span." *Human Development.* 34. 230-255.

6) Smith. J., & Freund. A.M. (2002). "The dynamics of possible selves in old age." *Journal of Gerontology,* 57B, P492-P-500.

7) Csikszentmihalyi, Mihaly, and Isabella Selega. Csikszentmihalyi. "A Life worth Living: Contributions to Positive Psychology." Series in *Positive Psychology.* Oxford: Oxford University Press, 2006.

8) Heider, F. (1958). *The Psychology of Interpersonal Relations.* New York: Wiley.

9) Weiten, Wayne, Margaret A. Lloyd, Dana Dunn, and Elizabeth Yost. *Hammer. Psychology Applied to Modern Life: Adjustment in the 21st Century.* 9th ed. Belmont, CA: Wadsworth, 2009.

10) Williams, Jean M. *Applied Sport Psychology: Personal Growth to Peak Performance.* 6th ed. Boston: McGraw-Hill Higher Education, 2010.

11) Kerr, J. H. *Counselling Athletes: Applying Reversal Theory.* London and New York: Routledge, 2001. P. 38

Chapter 2:

1) Nadal, Rafael, and John Carlin. *Rafa.* New York: Hyperion, 2011. P. 188

2) Cheadle, Carrie. *On Top of Your Game: Mental Skills to Maximize Your Athletic Performance.* Petaluma, CA.: Feed the Athlete Press, 2013. P. 185

3) "Interiors: Mint Dental/PCC Videos." www.youtube.com., Web. 2-11-2018.

Chapter 3:

1) Bryant, Cedric X., and Daniel J. Green. *ACE Lifestyle & Weight Management Coach Manual: The Ultimate Resource for Fitness Professionals.* 2nd ed. San Diego, CA: American Council on Exercise, 2011. P. 119, P. 185

2) Clark, Micheal. *NASM Essentials of Personal Fitness Training.* 6th ed. Burlington, MA: Jones & Bartlett Learning, 2018.

3) Duhigg, Charles. *The Power of Habit: Why We Do What We Do and How to Change It.* New York: Random House, 2012.

Chapter 4:

1) *NASM Essentials of Personal Fitness Training: Course Manual.* 3rd ed. Baltimore, MD: Lippincott Williams & Wilkins, 2008.

2) Weiten, Wayne, Margaret A. Lloyd, Dana Dunn, and Elizabeth Yost. Hammer. *Psychology Applied to Modern Life: Adjustment in the 21st Century.* 9th ed. Belmont, CA: Wadsworth, 2009.

3) Thill, John V., and Courtland L. Bovée. *Excellence in Business Communication.* 11th ed. Upper Saddle River: Pearson Education, 2015.

4) Carnegie, Dale. *How to Win Friends & Influence People: The Only Book You Need to Lead You to Success.* New York: Pocket Books, 2007. P. 143-144

Chapter 5:

1) McGrath, Joseph Edward, and Irwin Altman. *Social and Psychological Factors in Stress.* New York: Holt, Rinehart and Winston, 1970.

2) Weinberg, Robert Stephen., and Daniel Gould. *Foundations of Sport and Exercise Psychology.* 5th ed. Champaign, IL: Human Kinetics, 2011.

3) Cohen, Sheldon. *Behavior, Health, and Environmental Stress.* New York: Plenum Press, 1986.

4) Sarafino, Edward P. *Health Psychology: Biopsychosocial Interactions.* S.l.: John Wiley & Sons, 2006.

5) Orlick, Terry. *In Pursuit of Excellence: How to Win in Sport and Life through Mental Training.* 4th ed. Champaign: Human Kinetics, 2008. P. 264

6) Sapolsky, Robert M. *Why Zebras Dont Get Ulcers: An Updated Guide to Stress, Stress-related Diseases, and Coping.* 3rd ed. New York: W.H. Freeman, 2004.

7) LeDoux, Joseph E. Anxious: *Using the Brain to Understand and Treat Fear and Anxiety.* NY, NY: Penguin Books, 2016. P. 258

8) LeDoux, Joseph E. *The Emotional Brain: The Mysterious Underpinnings of Emotional Life.* New York: Simon & Schuster, 1998. P. 242

9) Sapolsky, Robert M. *Behave: The Biology of Humans at Our Best and Worst.* New York: Penguin Press, 2017. P. 143

10) Cozolino, Louis J. *The Neuroscience of Psychotherapy: Building and Rebuilding the Human Brain.* New York: Norton, 2002.

11) Karlin, W. A., Brondolo, E., & Schwartz, J. (2003). "Work-place social support and ambulatory cardiovascular activity in New York City traffic agents." *Psychosomatic Medicine,* 65, 165-176.

12) Wills, T. A., & Fegan, M.F. (2001). "Social networks and social support." In A. Baum, T.A. Revenson, & J.E. Singer (Eds.), *Handbook of Health Psychology*

13) Broman, C. L. (1993). "Social relationships and health related behavior." *Journal of Behavioral Medicine*, 16, 335-350

14) Cozolino, Louis J. *The Neuroscience of Human Relationships: Attachment and the Developing Social Brain.* 2nd ed. New York, NY: Norton & Company, 2014.

15) Ford, U. W., & Gordon, S. (1999). "Coping with sport injury: Resource loss and the role of social support." *Journal of Personal & Interpersonal Loss*, 4(3), 243-256.

16) Podlog, L., Wadey, R., Stark, A., Lochbaum, M., Hannon, J., & Newton, M. (2013). *An Adolescent Perspective on Injury Recovery and the Return to Sport. Psychology of Sport and Exercise*, 14(4), 437-446.

17) Wadey, R., Evans, L., Hanton, S., & Neil, R. (2012). "An examination of hardiness throughout the sport-injury process: A qualitative follow-up study." *British Journal of Health Psychology*, 17(4), 872-893.

Chapter 6:

1) Williams, Jean M. *Applied Sport Psychology: Personal Growth to Peak Performance.* 6th ed. Boston: McGraw-Hill Higher Education, 2010.

Chapter 7:

1) Murphy, Shane M. *The Sport Psych Handbook: A Complete Guide to Today's Best Mental Training Techniques.* Champaign, IL: Human Kinetics, 2005. P. 113

2) Orlick, Terry. *In Pursuit of Excellence: How to Win in Sport and Life through Mental Training.* 4th ed. Champaign: Human Kinetics, 2008.

3) Rock, David. *Your Brain at Work: Strategies for Overcoming Distraction, Regaining Focus and Working Smarter All Day Long.* New York: Harper Collins, 2010.

Chapter 8:

1) Ellis, A. (1982). "Self-direction in sport and life." In T. Orlick, J. Partington, & J, Salmela (Eds.), "Mental training for coaches

and athletes" (pp.10-17). Ottawa, ON: Coaching Association of Canada.

2) Williams, Jean M. *Applied Sport Psychology: Personal Growth to Peak Performance.* 6th ed. Boston: McGraw-Hill Higher Education, 2010.

Chapter 9:

1) Hammerness, Paul Graves., Margaret Moore, and John Hanc. *Organize Your Mind, Organize Your Life: Train Your Brain to Get More Done in Less Time.* Don Mills, Ont.: Harlequin, 2012. P. 33 P. 35

2) Achor, Shawn. *The Happiness Advantage: The Seven Principles That Fuel Success and Performance at Work.* London: Virgin, 2011. P.52-52 P. 60- 61 P. 97-98

3) Haidt, Jonathan. *The Happiness Hypothesis: Finding Modern Truth in Ancient Wisdom.* Basic Books, 2006. P. 94-96

4) Wiseman, Richard. *The Luck Factor: Changing Your Luck: Changing Your Life: The Four Essential Principles.* New York: Miramax Books, 2003.

5) Hill, Karen Lee. *Frameworks for Sport Psychologists: Enhancing Sport Performance.* Champaign, IL: Human Kinetics, 2001. P. 158

6) Hạnh, Nhất. *Being Peace.* Berkeley, CA: Parallax Press, 2005. P. 42

7) Weinberg, Robert Stephen., and Daniel Gould. *Foundations of Sport and Exercise Psychology.* 5th ed. Champaign, IL: Human Kinetics, 2011.

8) Orlick, Terry. *In Pursuit of Excellence: How to Win in Sport and Life through Mental Training.* 4th ed. Champaign: Human Kinetics, 2008. P. 44

9) Kerr, J. H. *Counselling Athletes: Applying Reversal Theory.* London and New York: Routledge, 2001. P. 37

10) Lipton, Bruce H. *The Biology of Belief: Unleashing the Power of Consciousness, Matter & Miracles.* Carlsbad, CA: Hay House, 2014. P. 93-95 P. 114

11) Bryant, Cedric X., and Daniel J. Green. *ACE Lifestyle & Weight Management Coach Manual: The Ultimate Resource for Fitness Professionals.* 2nd ed. San Diego, CA: American Council on Exercise, 2011. P. 46

Chapter 10:

1) Williams, Jean M. *Applied Sport Psychology: Personal Growth to Peak Performance.* 6th ed. Boston: McGraw-Hill Higher Education, 2010. P. 276

2) Murphy, Shane M. *The Sport Psych Handbook: A Complete Guide to Today's Best Mental Training Techniques.* Champaign, IL: Human Kinetics, 2005. P. 127 P. 133- 134

3) Orlick, Terry. *In Pursuit of Excellence: How to Win in Sport and Life through Mental Training.* 4th ed. Champaign: Human Kinetics, 2008. P. 105

4) Weinberg, Robert Stephen., and Daniel Gould. *Foundations of Sport and Exercise Psychology.* 5th ed. Champaign, IL: Human Kinetics, 2011.

Supplemental:

1) Missing Word Searches generated from https://mywordsearch. com, Web. 7-11-2018

2) Hour Glass Drawings: Glenn Krupka

Find the Missing Motivational Ingredient

```
G  S  P  E  C  I  F  I  C  C  H  O  O  S  E  Z  G  Z  R  A
P  O  S  C  B  A  G  V  A  A  V  L  X  R  V  T  H  E  A  O
D  Z  A  O  N  K  A  N  N  L  O  M  N  G  W  P  B  T  C  X
J  S  C  L  B  R  L  B  O  R  L  C  T  R  S  E  B  L  T  L
M  O  A  Z  S  T  A  Q  T  I  A  C  X  Z  A  H  Y  H  I  D
Y  M  K  W  T  P  V  N  T  C  T  V  Y  W  R  T  J  N  V  Z
O  E  B  S  J  R  O  Q  E  Z  P  P  A  X  L  R  F  O  A  Q
S  M  N  Z  O  C  O  K  V  H  C  R  E  I  E  N  T  F  T  H
T  I  O  D  K  E  R  P  V  J  E  E  B  C  N  G  M  Z  I  P
R  T  I  X  J  F  W  L  P  N  H  A  R  B  R  B  P  P  O  E
E  E  T  F  O  C  U  S  E  U  T  Q  U  O  M  E  P  U  N  R
S  M  A  T  N  Y  O  S  E  N  S  I  A  B  Z  C  P  X  V  S
S  O  X  W  V  J  S  B  U  M  S  L  W  G  B  D  G  S  R  O
P  T  A  I  O  F  S  O  X  R  Z  V  A  K  Z  Y  N  H  U  N
E  I  L  K  S  I  C  I  R  F  Y  H  I  I  K  V  N  A  R  A
Y  O  E  Q  G  C  B  I  G  L  Y  Q  I  Z  C  I  Q  Q  V  L
T  N  R  W  A  U  W  Z  U  E  G  D  U  O  V  O  P  P  E  Z
O  S  Y  U  N  C  M  D  Y  V  M  E  G  T  B  X  S  M  P  C
M  Z  G  O  N  E  F  O  N  F  Y  R  S  N  X  X  H  R  O  H
X  I  W  E  U  Q  I  D  F  R  D  H  L  S  L  Y  V  G  M  T
```

Word List:

Accountability	Control	Perception	Specific
Activation	Emotions	Personal	Stress
Awareness	Focus	Relaxation Time	
Choose	Goals	Social Support	

Find the Missing Motivational Ingredient

```
P D W O R H I P P O C A M P U S Y D C D
A S S E N E V I T R E S S A T W X Z Y Q
Q S S N D M P C Y N J C E C H V I B B H
V R Q B A A U H O A A O I G O S M D E F
F G N U U A D W C S H M T P U O I H H U
H C Y N G Z U T C E Q P I A G B U X A F
X L I T W U I D Q E J E R N H M L T V R
I G O M I O Y Q C T P T O T T O Y F I B
D G P E N L J E G M X E I S S T K C O D
E Y F L U P I D C M E N R E O I Q U R F
N G F F R I R B D N V C P J E V F S E D
D W R K K A M X I O E E Q R Y A D E W P
R A M R P M L A H S R R N D Z T L B Q P
I H H R H E F U G C N B E E A I F Y L T
T W S G Z V X C X E V O L H N O Q T Q S
E G S A J M P F C H R J P G D N C E R A
S N P W B O N O D P V Y S S E A G I F D
I H W D Y E Z S P P R H S L E Y X X U R
C F F W J Q E U T O E F Z T C R G N K Z
K D G C L G Y T N I A T R E C N U A D R
```

Word List:

Action   Behavior   Hippocampus   Responsibility

Adherence   Competence   Imagery   Thoughts

Anxiety   Dendrites   Motivation   Uncertainty

Assertiveness   Feelings   Priorities

Find the Missing Motivational Ingredient

```
A  F  E  C  O  R  E  M  O  T  I  V  A  T  O  R  S  A  K  N
T  R  N  F  P  W  U  P  Z  Y  G  B  G  P  E  X  U  W  O  R
T  S  N  O  I  T  A  M  R  I  F  F  A  L  G  S  B  I  T  K
A  C  L  Q  B  G  I  H  C  D  O  F  B  T  S  C  T  X  N  E
I  H  O  Z  U  A  R  E  U  R  D  A  W  E  M  A  C  Y  E  L
N  D  D  N  I  M  P  M  Q  I  R  B  N  V  R  B  O  G  M  J
A  N  C  T  F  Z  F  C  Y  U  D  D  C  T  R  S  M  X  E  K
B  R  P  N  O  I  G  E  S  M  E  S  N  M  S  G  M  W  V  V
L  P  F  Z  O  R  D  A  C  T  Z  E  M  Q  Z  F  I  U  E  D
E  B  A  Z  J  I  E  E  A  N  C  X  K  H  S  A  T  E  I  F
K  L  J  B  Y  M  T  L  N  N  V  C  I  J  I  I  M  O  H  A
H  E  H  Y  Z  Y  E  A  O  C  J  M  J  A  C  S  E  P  C  N
G  B  G  S  N  R  B  C  C  J  E  E  V  T  O  A  N  T  A  T
P  Q  G  Q  W  N  F  F  S  I  R  P  R  U  E  B  T  M  T  E
S  T  I  M  U  L  U  S  C  O  N  T  R  O  L  T  G  I  W  C
A  R  P  P  I  U  C  M  C  A  D  U  B  E  G  M  L  S  Q  D
S  D  S  Y  V  R  A  J  A  Y  H  R  M  R  T  R  P  T  I  E
O  N  Y  S  N  F  W  B  V  S  D  C  H  M  I  X  T  I  Y  N
J  R  S  N  O  I  T  C  A  R  T  S  I  D  O  B  J  C  Y  T
K  N  O  I  T  A  C  I  D  E  D  P  U  Y  L  C  C  T  G  S
```

Word List:

Achievement   Commitment   Core Motivators   Optimistic

Affirmations   Communication   Dedication   Relatedness

Antecedents   Concentration   Distractions   Stimulus   Control

Attainable   Confidence   Measurable

Find the Missing Motivational Ingredient

```
P  R  A  C  T  I  C  E  X  M  J  V  L  Y  N  U  T  F  Y  B
B  S  R  H  Y  C  T  F  U  E  G  N  D  W  G  A  B  A  W  F
P  D  N  U  W  O  O  Y  I  U  K  E  Z  Z  U  Q  T  M  X  D
M  P  A  O  Y  Z  L  U  N  O  I  S  I  V  S  Y  Y  H  Y  U
H  E  I  N  I  D  Z  V  N  S  W  Y  S  S  V  C  P  E  C  Z
J  C  Z  N  M  T  Q  R  T  T  X  J  R  D  N  E  T  U  H  Y
G  N  U  O  N  I  U  B  M  L  E  Q  U  E  O  Y  J  R  A  U
C  N  E  H  N  O  L  B  Y  I  H  R  T  G  P  O  S  I  N  K
K  W  I  X  X  T  V  S  I  Z  K  S  I  O  I  E  M  S  G  T
T  K  W  S  Z  E  D  A  Z  R  I  E  S  N  I  B  N  T  E  S
J  L  R  G  U  M  M  L  T  S  T  I  U  G  G  B  L  I  L  V
D  J  E  O  O  C  Y  K  N  I  T  T  E  B  D  Z  H  C  D  Q
R  X  F  L  U  L  O  O  L  I  V  T  A  T  I  W  O  K  O  B
X  G  R  F  R  M  C  F  V  U  A  E  I  U  L  C  R  P  H  W
N  L  A  Q  X  P  D  E  E  R  W  P  G  G  I  V  C  V  A  W
K  X  M  F  S  D  K  B  T  R  T  A  L  O  C  K  I  C  B  Y
R  J  I  W  J  C  K  S  P  T  Z  P  G  I  I  L  T  R  I  L
P  Y  N  Z  Q  N  E  B  A  H  I  E  V  D  Q  I  M  I  T  T
F  V  G  X  S  G  M  J  N  L  H  D  D  K  C  E  A  E  S  J
O  B  E  L  I  E  F  M  V  R  J  K  S  V  M  T  K  O  D  A
```

Word List:

Attributions   Countering   Moods   Reframing

Belief   Habits   Positive   Strategies

Change   Heuristic   Practice   Vision

Consistency   Innovative   Refocusing

End of Book Motivational Tip:

This tip comes in the form of a physical reminder. It is something I have utilized for at least a year, a motivational wristband! I have a yellow wristband that has the words, "Keep Moving!" engraved in it. As we know from Chapter 1, the word *motivation* is derived from the Latin word "movere," meaning "to move," so what a great reminder to ask ourselves throughout our busy day, "Am I motivated, today, mentally and physically? If not, what motivational ingredients do I need to incorporate into my day, so that I have the best recipe for success?"

Be the Best of Whatever You Are

If you can't be a pine on the top of the hill,
Be a scrub in the valley but be
The best little scrub by the side of the hill;
Be a bush if you can't be a tree.
If you can't be a bush be a bit of grass,
Some highway happier make;
If you can't be a muskee then just be a bass-
But the liveliest bass in the lake.
We can't all be captains, we've got to be crew;
There's something for all of us here.
There's big work to do and there's lesser to do,
And the task you must do is the near.
If you can't be a highway then be a trail;
If you can't be the sun be a star.
It isn't by size that you win or you fail,
Be the best of whatever you are!

Douglas Malloch

About the Author

Robert Kirby's educational experience includes a BA in Psychology and a Graduate Certificate in Sport Psychology from John F. Kennedy University, one-year marketing study at Portland Community College, and numerous personal training certifications. He has a background in personal training and health coaching. Robert's website, robertkirbytraining.com, provides an abundance of healthy tips and recipes. He lives by the philosophy, "Awareness and insight lead to reflection, which fuels goal-directed action."

CPSIA information can be obtained
at www.ICGtesting.com
Printed in the USA
FSHW011821110119
54935FS